UNDERSTANDING
SOMEONE ELSE
FOR A CHANGE

OR

OUTSIGHT IS BETTER THAN INSIGHT

ALFRED FIREMAN, MD

with Patrica Vaughn

Illustrated by Jeff Whitehurst

Dedicated to all my groups because
several are more beautiful than one
and we are more interesting than I.

ISBN: 978-0-9833376-2-1

Production Services:
Populore Publishing Company, Morgantown, West Virginia,
with cover design by Jenna Britton

Contents

Preface

This is not a book of therapy. It is an exposition of the thesis that looking at others in the world and understanding them is as crucial to securing and maintaining one's own mental health as is the inner-directed contemplation of the self.

What we are about to produce is an eclectic ordering of the best "how to understand somebody else" material which has been gleaned from an overall education and practice in clinical psychiatry.

Our teachers have been primarily classical Freudian and neo-Freudian professors with a heavy overlay of Sullivanians and existential West European psychiatrists. But you shall not be spared the sayings of Confucius; the chant of the Holy Rollers; the insights of Erma Bombeck, Gail Sheehy or Judith Viorst if they have been tested in practice and found worthwhile on the solid turf of "It works, Doctor, and I feel better."

No one will be saved through this text, but no reader who has made an honest study effort will be unable to say at some point in his reading, "Not a bad idea; I think I'll try that," or "No wonder Charlie or Cynthia acts that way; in that case I think I shall act otherwise myself." Or, "Now I see that I also behave similarly when my space is threatened—when I am challenged to be intimate—when I am afraid."

In medieval Italy forceps were kept by physicians in the castles for the aristocracy while the peasants were allowed to tear their pelvises and otherwise have their bodies mutilated through "natural childbirth" without benefit of the scientific and technological breakthrough of metal forceps.

Analogously, we believe that psychiatrists have the intellectual forceps necessary for comprehending the social intercourse of the average person, gleaned and extrapolated from careers in understanding so-called patients who have had so-called nervous breakdowns. Instead of setting apart their material in the formal literature of the profession and exclusively directing their efforts to the care of the ill, we believe that psychiatrists should endeavor to "go public." It is in fact our belief that American medicine has withheld its professional leadership in preventive medicine by adhering to an outdated premise that "unsupervised" medical education of the public violates the ethics of "not advertising."

This book is not called "How to be a Psychiatrist in Ten Easy Lessons." It addresses itself to the problems of the average individual conveying how the expertise of the psychiatrist, the specialist in human relationships and human understanding, can be translated and rendered accessible to lay readers to facilitate the normal conduct of their interpersonal life.

Just as biochemists and nutritionists in their laboratories initially determined the minimum daily requirements of the various substances necessary to health and well-being and then delivered their discoveries to the manufacturers of now-fortified bread, so does this text attempt to transfer the experience and scholarship of psychiatric principles and techniques to you, the reader, for a more agile and comfortable experience in your interpersonal space.

We expect to facilitate this process by examining our own and others' roadblocks and resistances for securing satisfying relationships by defining alternatives and by uncovering our less apparent relationship desires.

We will consider relationships with friends, family, lovers, spouses, children, etc. We will offer viewpoints on each type of relationship with a view toward increasing options for success and happiness in each. We will first and most importantly learn how to observe and listen to others.

However advantageous such an enterprise may be for those who are understood, our book is coincidentally based on the belief that an equally important reason for understanding others is our personal benefit.

For we have discovered that understanding others proves often to be the best and most direct route for becoming more aware of ourselves.

Thus our theme emerges: outsight is better than insight. We shall argue *that the skills of outsight have too long gone undeveloped because we have taken relationships for granted,* bowing to culturally and traditionally established patterns of our total society and whatever subgroups we belong to.

In our developmental years we were all programmed to have specific definitions and concepts about the nature of certain relationships. We were taught how a child should relate to a parent and vice versa; the kinds of things we "should" do for and with each other. Most of our attitudes and patterns of relating were imprinted on us as children. We learned the ropes hit-or-miss ... but in time, learn we did.

The problem is that much of what we so painfully learned turns out to be inappropriate for our experiences as adults in peer adult relationships. And even when we have recognized this, most of us continue to operate on repetitious compulsions rather than moving courageously toward a newer, more satisfying mode.

Relationships in today's world must be viewed as ongoing and dynamic rather than static.

Like our natural environment, we humans are also in "interpersonal" motion. Thus static non-changing and non-growing relationships can no longer satisfy most of us.

Does this mean the end of security in relationships? No, but it does mean that more of us are demanding that our relationships be based on contemporary agreements rather than accidents of birth, marriage licenses and inherited social responsibilities. For most modern relationships to last and be satisfying they must be based on processes of growth and give and take—less on tradition, more on understanding. In order for participants to prosper in their relationships they must become aware of the less apparent, though often more profound purposes and goals of their communion. They must also understand the differences between freedom of choice in relationships and license to "let it all hang out."

Does understanding dispose to better relationships? Not necessarily, for it may serve to facilitate the ending of a relationship already begun, or discourage us from the pursuit of one which we might previously have opted for.

Once we understand others, we may surely better choose whether to relate to them or not—and if so, how.

Few among us will opt for total isolation. We may choose to limit our relationships to certain spheres of our lives (only in business; only in marriage; only parent/child relationships; only friendships) but most people want some type of relating with others.

The trick is to develop new patterns of relationships that are responsible, to our own needs and to the needs of those we relate to!

If, once we understand others, we find that current relationships will not fill our needs, we may opt to develop new ones. But to choose relationships in an aware, willing and committed way, each participant must begin from a knowledge of his or her own purposes, identity and goals.

So, understanding others can be a vital instrument in securing intimacy; for in the new experience of understanding them (and ourselves secondarily) there follows a now special opportunity to engage them for a communion and sharing, rooted in our primitive awareness that two is better than one for pleasure, and that the dyad has more survival value for the participants than each alone.

We all think we know who we are and what we want. In truth, most things we say we are and want are all too often what "they" said we wanted, and bear little resemblance to what is going on with us now. Likewise do we all too frequently invite those about us to become players from our past rather than allow them to be now and originally present.

If you want to know yourself, we recommend outsight rather than insight as the best available tool for such self-awareness, and suggest that from understanding others *primarily as they relate to you* are you able to understand the true basis of your experiences of pleasure and pain.

Remember, though, that the understood others are no more likely to change than remain the same for it. So be warned that giving one's understanding to another, even when conveyed benevolently, does not change him or her and may be just as often experienced as an intrusion into privacy.

Our purpose, however, will not be frustrated, for it is we who are more likely to be changed in our relationships as we observe others and understand them. The true theme of this book is that understanding someone else is as good, or better, for us as for them.

However, an extremely useful technique for changing yourself is understanding others because your behavior is as likely to change in response to what you are and understand in others as it is from what you see and understand in yourself. Our purpose is growth and improvement of self, not the growth and improvement of others.

While it may be a virtue and a joy to participants to have an understanding relationship with each other, it must remain a voluntary experience. For to trespass with our understanding into the space of another without invitation is in a most critical sense an invasion of privacy.

Our book does not begin with the premise that the reader is a likeable or loveable or reachable person. It says, "Look, very likely your personal problems to a significant extent reflect your inability to get along with others, so let us show you how to understand them a bit better." Our alternate premise is that most personal problems are interpersonal and that it is only upon reflection and consideration of the significant and special other persons in our lives that we secure sure focus and proper appreciation of ourselves.

Introduction: Confessions of a Psychiatrist

As a psychiatrist I have been taught to understand somebody else—not for a change but in a consistent professional fashion. My training began as a student of the human body, and the lessons of medical school and internship were crucial for later considerations of the physical basis for the behavior of all persons. The former gave me knowledge to diagnose and technique to alter the bodies of sick patients; the latter the experience of having their nakedness entrusted to me and the responsibility of utilizing my knowledge in a professionally responsible and helpful way.

Whereas taking care of the whole patient was the goal, the core practical requirements of not missing a diagnosis; properly suturing the laceration; adjusting acid base balance; removing lumps and killing bacteria and viruses, were so compelling that the total person possessed of the illness was often lost in the enterprise.

It was nice to find him again in my psychiatric residency and renew my understanding of patients through a core profound interrogation and interaction with them as persons.

It was, paradoxically, often disconcerting to my patients that (1) we psychiatrists were not surgeons; and (2) that rather than the laying on of hands to alter their emotionally distraught lives (the surrender of their sickness to our healing), we preferred the shared enterprise of working together.

I was not searching for the source organ of their chief complaints and present illnesses; I was not preoccupied with their exposure to infection or physical trauma, soreness, swelling and redness had given way to anxiety and depression as primary complaints, and understanding became interpersonal rather than subject-physician treating object-body-patient. However, at random moments of rebellion in my psychoanalytically oriented residency training program, I questioned whether an intellectual deceit had been perpetrated upon me—for my teachers seemed to have replaced id, ego and superego for pancreas, thyroid and cricoid cartilage; and conscious and unconscious psychodynamics for the hemodynamics of bile, blood and lymph.

Patients and their problems all too often remained elusive under such a theoretical superstructure. Patients did hold tenaciously to their status quo symptoms and

1

surrendered their hidden inner selves only with the most rigorous and ingenious reluctance. I could not allow this to be explained with psychoanalytic one-liners as if there really were such things as ids and egos. I felt that the metaphors originally meant to enrich the meaning of persons had replaced them and that, in the presence of people in pain, helpers were playing word games.

Deep psychotherapy had come to mean to me psychiatrists being in over their heads, and what seemed necessary now was a scuba outfit instead of tidy-blue-shirt-and-pastel-sport-coat. I realized that all too many psychodynamic formulations of patients were no more personal than talking about their body parts.

I was sure there had to be more to it than this, so I began to read Harry Stack Sullivan, Ludwig Binswanger, and Medard Boss. For, to the question, "Do you understand what I mean?" I was often replying, "I see that your id wishes are conflicted with your superego restraints and that this conflict has produced anxiety which has undergone a transformation to phobia of closed spaces." I was told that in order for this interpretive message to produce insight and have worth, it must be part of an interpersonal relationship in which I had secured a therapeutic alliance with the patient's observing ego. This was otherwise referred to as a positive transference. Then to the rescue came Elvin Semrad, psychoanalyst par excellence, whose simple wisdom would melt the ice of psychiatric jargon. "Folks will be folks" he advised us and, "No interpretation can be heavier than the bond of trust which precedes it." He would then remind us of the old-time jungle movies where Tarzan swung over the ravine, holding fast to a single length of vine, then returned precariously hand over hand, repeating this until the footbridge was completed, capable of bearing not only his weight but also that of his companion.

The complexity of securing such a relationship may be likened to the dilemma of porcupines huddled together at the brook side on an unpleasantly cold winter morning. Convinced that their body warmth could be shared if they remained together, they appreciated that they must do something about their spines in order to secure the necessary closeness.

This task, so metaphorically simplified, is enormously complicated. Yet this book has ambition to presume that whereas you may hurt the one you love (with your spines) as you proceed toward intimacy, you are less likely and less severely to do so as you master the lessons of our text.

Just as a psychiatrist's success with his patient results more from the building of the conveyance of the interpersonal relationship than it does from his delivery of psychological truths to the patient (which the patient will surely not hear, except in the interpersonal climate of trust), so it is in all relationships.

So come with us in the next one hundred or so pages into the interpersonal space. Learn the vocabulary not of objects or bodies perceived, nor of cells analyzed, but of folks interacting with folks. Quest with us to understand not just who, what and why they are and how they fit into our world, but how we fit into theirs as well, and be assured that in the quest you, like thousands of others so guided, will exclaim not "There but for the grace of God go I," but "Here with the gift and trust of outsight go we."

· · ·

1

Who's Crazy?

*"The will is all powerful, imperious, without purpose of direction.
We do not want a thing because we reason, we find reason for things
because we want them. Mind invents logic for the whim of the will."*

—*Schopenhauer*
Neurosis as a Solution

Late 19th century neurologists rejected patients as sufferers of true diseases when no discernible neuropathology could be discovered for their look-alike symptoms. These people were labeled as malingerers until Charcot, a French neurologist of great personal prestige and charisma, declared that these individuals were also to be considered "sick," and in need of physician treatment and understanding for the new disease he called hysteria.

That simple fact of medical history opened up for Freud, one of Charcot's disciples, the opportunity to found a whole new sub-specialty of medicine called psychoanalysis. For Freud took back to Vienna Charcot's argument and began searching out not the missing germs or other infectious agents which had deranged the thinking of his patients and compromised their ability to test reality, but theoretical forces in their so-called unconscious psyches, searching for the noxious ideas buried beneath the scabs and scar tissue of suppression and repression. With his own medical authority gained through his neurological experiments in the fields of aphasia and cocaine anesthesia, Freud was able to rally to his side a devoted group of other physicians and to publish his work in medical and neurological journals.

However, today it no longer seems appropriate for the medical monopoly to care for such "look-alike" patients. The folks so troubled today have every right to reach out to other kinds of professionals as well as to their friends and neighbors, who can provide legitimate and honest services for another experience—not one of therapeutic understanding but of friendly understanding.

Although the early psychoanalytic literature is extraordinarily insightful for comprehending the human experience, it is no more "medical" than any other

5

strong philosophical, sociological or political treatise on the questions of human behavior. For while such painful symptoms and unusual modes of behavior as those called "mental illness" may be similar to that seen in conditions known to be caused by abnormal or sick brain cells, this similarity does not justify the exclusive use of the medical model for all painful feelings or socially unacceptable or perverse behavior.

There does exist, of course, a legitimate and proper territory for medical practitioners in the healing of mental and emotional illnesses. But our essential position is that the majority of so-called mentally ill people are not medically troubled or disabled individuals. The era of look-alike diseases is about over, reduced to faddism and cultism, and devotion to its precepts endures only in the minds of those ancestor worshippers still residing in the downtown office buildings of Manhattan, Cambridge and Los Angeles who still fuss over membership requirements to their bankrupt institutes, content to think that all resistance to their poorly aging arguments is the neurotic acting out of tyrants, saboteurs, heretics and "bad guys."

The exclusive medical model and argument for understanding others is socially and scientifically untenable and culturally outdated. Psychotherapy, good advice, rehabilitation, working things out and self-actualization are experiences which can be realized through the efforts of a much larger group of professionally competent people than medicine has deigned. We carry this argument one step further by suggesting that whereas treating others may remain the prerogative of professionals, understanding them can be taught to most of us.

In so doing we encourage everyone to return to the role of significant helping and friendly others without hazard of malpractice litigation on the one hand or violation of proper territorial imperatives on the other.[1] We do not disallow the crucial need for first-class professional M.D. psychiatrists to treat the most seriously and assuredly deranged, irrational, symptom-ridden psychotic citizens of our community. This aside, however, untold millions of others surely could profit from the two experiences of (1) being able to understand others better, and (2) as a consequence of this, becoming more aware of themselves in the process.

---

1   A few more words on the notion of sick or well, and the suitability of therapy rather than scorn for patients as malingerer: We seem to have come full circle on this topic. On a recent popular TV program, when the villain had just been found guilty of a most heinous offense, our hero medical examiner, one Quincy by name, looked at him with all of the disgust of an 18th century keeper of the hell gate and scowled, "You're sick," with such disgust as to blur the horizontal reception. Alas he had come full circle, for now "sick" meant vile and perverse—not only not well but not human.

As Nietzsche said, "One who is unable to loosen his own chains may yet be a redeemer for his friends. I and me are always too earnestly in conversation. How could it be endured if there were not a friend? The third one is the cork which preventeth the conversation of the two from sinking into the depths."

The only necessary provision is that the territory of the observer be neutral. This doesn't mean that the observed person is reduced to an object or thing. It means that the emotional distance we are more likely to apply to others than to ourselves provides the virtue of a less passionate and thereby more realistic appreciation of their behavior and needs.

A most important corollary of this is that a careful listening and understanding of others is one of the best techniques for achieving self-awareness. Outsight produces insight!

In group psychotherapy sessions patients are counseled that their therapy hours are exercises in advanced listening.

When one finishes a statement in conversation he is too accustomed to look at agreement as validation that he was understood—and when others disagree he is more likely to retort, "But you don't understand."

Here we see a colloquialism turned into a proverb: "If you had understood, you would have agreed." But this is hardly the case.

From two people understanding each other and yet not agreeing (as opposed to two individuals "yessing" each other into blandness) there is more likely to develop enriching new truths.

One early discovery we often make of others is that very often symptoms of illness, personal discomfort and self-defeating ways of behaving, though in and of themselves noxious and painful—serve the two-fold function of being both a solution to some problems while being problems in themselves, i.e., while in a state of overwhelming and devastating anxiety I may raise my right hand and commit a terrible crime of assault or murder. Or, so provoked with fear and rage, I may solve the problem by developing a conversion paralysis of my right arm. The following day I may then present myself to a physician with a limp and flaccid arm which he may define as "my problem." One layer below that simple approach is the alternate truth: that the paralysis of my arm is a solution to my problem of being otherwise unable to cope with my raw hostility and homicidal inclinations. Were it not paralyzed, that arm would have been used to commit an act my conscience could not condone.

Such a simple insight as this[2] provides a vast source of data for use in the endeavor of understanding all human relationships—the hidden meanings which explain the otherwise irrational: *the hidden purpose which makes the worthless, valuable.*

As we look upon our neighbors using this concept of the necessity of symptoms, we achieve a more empathetic state of mind than is available when viewing them as having *surrendered* to those symptoms, be they phobia, conversion hysteria, psychosomatic disability, or obsessive and compulsive thinking or acting. While it may be inappropriate to tense up when boarding an elevator and to instead elect to climb twelve flights of stairs rather than ensure the pain and suffering of being in that closed space, it *does* have a primitive logic and can be understood.

The solution may now be judged as less adequate than the more usual and customary approaches to solving certain life problems and we may therefore be guided to look for deeper sources for the action which may lie one step beyond the manifest. There surely may be no *rational* reason, for instance, to fear the closed space of an elevator. We need only expand our thinking one orbit beyond the simple to find the other so-called latent meaning: that when in a closed space some people are brought to a heightened awareness of their own rage because they are in a setting in which flight to a neutral space is physically prohibited.

It is not that the elevator will come crashing to the ground from a broken cable (which would be fear rather than a phobia—an important difference), but that rage will soar higher and faster than the elevator ascends, and that in this closed space, anger will become intolerable. In this way we may learn that seldom is it from others or other things that people develop the symptoms of illness and discomfort, but primarily from their own conflicted inability to deal with how they have been "made" to feel.

As soon as we come to know this we can learn to view others differently, and therefore act differently and soon thereafter perhaps feel differently toward them.

Each one of us may possess our own special deviation. Whereas there are only so many measures on the hematocrit and blood sugar scales, *there is infinite variety to human aberration*—all of which may be called "sick" and thus generate a treatment response.

Too often that which is labeled "sick" is merely individual … it is the punishment dealt by an unimaginative and rigid society to all who march to different drummers, even when the marcher is the harbinger of a new and better way of

---

2   Derived from those marvelous case studies of Freud and Breuer during their earliest collaboration in 1889–1895.

living. History is replete with examples of untolerated progress and the martyr-dom of those who attempted to share their visions with the world. To laud such individuals centuries after their time is merely an apology for our former limita-tions and fears. A truly civilized culture would respond with at least immediate tolerance.

Now not everyone who exists outside the mold of his or her current cultural expectations is a genius or a forerunner of a new life style. But many are, and it is impossible to discern who is and who isn't from the parameters of our cultural codes. If we are to allow a flowering of full human potential, we must develop an openness to those who are "other than" and a respectful interest in their otherness.

If you really want to understand others, you have to be "there" with as many other people as you can. Our first step then is to increase our interest in others and thereby enrich our own humanity.

The argument "If I can do it, so can he" (so frequently mobilized against those whose behavior we consider shallow, weak, neurotic and ineffectual) will not be indulged in this book. The last thing the other whom we choose to under-stand requires is a comparative recitation of his frailties and our strengths; his malice and our benevolence; his liabilities and our virtue. We will seldom ask, "Why can't other people be more like me?" We will more frequently ask, "How can I comprehend why others are as they are, rather than like me?"

When we look at the manifestations of apparently aberrant actions as *solutions to problems* as well as problems, we are in a much better position to search for an understanding of their underlying determinants, having recognized that however inadequate the neurotic solution may be and whatever new problems it creates, it began taking the doer from more to less pain. In separating the doer from the deed, we and he must rediscover that pain.

Thus the path to change often includes more pain. While such a journey is generally mediated by a psychiatrist for his patients, it may often be traversed in friendship by helping others. The lessons and experiences of the psychiatrist in this endeavor has utility for all of us who think that for another to change his way to ways more suitable to our needs is but a simple, painless task.

Reason may be the friend of science and the essential instrument for under-standing the orbit of planets or the nature of matter, but it is not necessarily the best reference for understanding the behavior of others. It is our *reason* which we *apply* in understanding others' beliefs, *but there need be nothing reasonable about beliefs* though belief accounts for substantial portions of our behavior.

In explaining why Freud left hypnosis for the method of free association, the story is told of the little man who, responding to an earlier hypnotic suggestion, opened his umbrella in Charcot's laboratory. He was pressed to explain his unusual behavior. After a whole series of preposterous and face-saving silly explanations (called rationalizations) he was finally, in exhaustion, able to tease out of his unconsciousness the hidden repressed suggestion. A small step for a little French gentleman in a Paris laboratory in 1884 but a leap for the readers of this text in 1978 as well as the birth of psychoanalysis.

For you will soon come to know that not only French gentlemen under hypnotic suggestions perform compulsive human behavior, but also that all of us—under suggestions and beliefs placed by mother, father, sister and school teacher in the days of our early childhood and adolescence—display vast areas of irrational behavior, which we very often defend with such similar nonsense rather than confess their true source, i.e., "My mother said it was so and that's why I believe it."

We should be as flexible in disengaging from these arguments as we expect natives in Samoa to be in converting to Christianity or peasants in Pakistan to adopt boiling their water in time of plague.

Continuing our search for the hidden premises behind others' behavior, I am reminded of a recent group psychotherapy session in which Mary asked those present not to smoke. Laura replied, "How can someone who has lived with a man for 2 1/2 years dare ask somebody else not to smoke?" A conflict of mistaken premises. Mary did not want pollutants in her lungs or clothing, and Laura took the admonishment to be on moral grounds.

We are forced to inquire, in cases where communications are so poor, into the individual philosophies underlying each action. But it is amazing how many people are hard-pressed to define their philosophy beyond such one-line responses as, "Yes, I believe in God," "No, I'm against abortion," "Yes, I believe in euthanasia." One reason that arguments on religion and politics often degenerate to screaming matches is that, soon after their onset, one or another of the partners is confronted with the shallow rivers of reason on which they have chosen to move the cargo of their argument. The folly of the encounter is that whereas arguments must be rooted to logic, beliefs may prevail free of such constraint.

Remember when we were kids, if anyone said something about our mothers how terrible it was and what wrath could ensue? Well, it works the same way here. Our mothers and fathers handed us our culture and our beliefs and said it was good and right. So if someone says, "Hey, kid," or "Hey, adult, what your mother told you is false," we have been known to take it damned seriously, even violently! But why? Why shouldn't new others be able to tell us that our mother may have made a mistake? Anthropologists do this all the time when they go to cultures other than their own. I believe that we hold to our contemporary "sophisticated" vows and beliefs with the same primitive mechanisms and tenacity that aborigines hold to theirs.

We humans, who have so recently come by the use of our evolutionary enlarged cerebral cortices, try to demonstrate our advance up the phylogenetic line by flashing our reason at less fit neighbors, both in our own and in other species—yet the fact is that it is not necessarily the best reference for understanding the behavior of others. Beliefs need not be reasonable.

However aware we may become of the underlying beliefs and motives of others, we must keep in mind that *"Neither I nor my offerings are necessarily good for, nor is it your responsibility to meet my needs for intimacy."*

These premises constitute an excellent beginning for an interpersonal enterprise. A first piece of interpersonal business then to be transacted is this: Can we agree on why we have convened? Are we likely prospects to know, care and respond to each other or to teach, work or travel with one another?

Too bad we haven't learned to respect and stalk our intimate interests with the same dedication that we do our enemies! We use the word "learned" here advisedly for the whole point of this presentation is to appreciate that such a project can be learned.

Consider the story of the migration of a sparrow from his New Hampshire summer residence to his winter home in Florida:

Having gotten a tardy start he finds himself beset with fog and rainstorms over North Georgia and, losing ground and stamina, abruptly falls into a pasture. As he sighs his last breath of life, a grazing mother Guernsey cow drawn to his death, rustling, furnishes him a cover of excrement with sufficient warmth and nourishment to sustain him. Relieved and restored in the early morning of the following day, he begins to peck his way forward into the light of morning and with the first glimpses of sunshine squeaks his ode of rejuvenation. A cat in a nearby barn, thus alerted, comes to investigate the noise and after scratching at the dung pile discovers the sparrow and eats him. The messages here are simple: (1) everyone who shits on you is not your enemy; (2) everyone who takes shit off you is not your friend; and (3) when you're in shit up to your eyeballs, keep your mouth shut.

This story illustrates the argument that people are all too often not what they seem nor do they mean what we believe we have heard them say. This story is offered to point out the need to achieve skills in diminishing the likelihood that we will relate to "seeming" as if it were "being," and specifically in the interpersonal sphere as opposed to our assessment of things or objects.

It would be preposterous on any but the most lofty metaphysical mountaintop to inquire "I wonder what that rock means by sitting there" as opposed to asking how it got there. In the interpersonal sphere, meaning is complicated and enriched by the factors of motive and presupposition. However, the question, "I wonder what he means by that," is that key question; and this book is designed to facilitate coming to a more efficient and workable answer than would probably be achieved without such an education.

> *"I would advise you to set aside your therapeutic ambitions and try to understand what is happening; when you have done that, therapeutics will take care of itself."*
> —*Sigmund Freud*

When to Call the Doctor

Because mistaken premises are a major stumbling block to understanding the behavior of others, let's look at how we decide that others are crazy. For instance, we would likely conclude that anyone who believes he or she is Anthony or Cleopatra and patterns behavior to that premise is crazy or deluded. Thereafter we are likely to monitor our responses to such "crazy" people in any one of a number of different ways. We may initially try logic: "You see, Sarah, you can't be Cleopatra because this is Pawtucket, Rhode Island, in 1978 and she lived in ancient Egypt before Christ was born."

In handling our frustration at the inevitable failure of such an argument we may explore kindness: "Poor darling," we may reflect, "she knows not what she rants," and then assign her to a mental hospital or tolerate her at home in the attic or guest room.

Occasionally her refusal to behave herself and to see the correctness of our calculation that she is not Cleopatra generates an angry and rejecting response and we may give up and leave her sitting there. Or, if she persists in jarring our sense of logic and order with her insistence, we may have to hit or constrain her and at least get her out of the way of our children and loved ones. Throughout, however, our understanding is that she clearly is crazy and not normal.

But what about the less clear-cut situation when another person insists on behaving on a belief or premise that is not so obviously unrealistic and thus not subject to clear logical refutation? What do we do when another's behavior seriously compromises the conduct of our mutual business, such as when a marriage becomes drained by the malignant suspicions of our mate? The worn husband or wife may dutifully provide an in-depth itinerary of his/her day, day after day, listing where and with whom time was spent and which topics were discussed at each stopping place.

For any of you who have been so misjudged, you know that such an effort produces little more than your fatigue and your doubter's increased frustration. It should occur to you to say after such an exhausting project, "I wonder why he/she continues to feel and act that way in the face of all the evidence to the contrary?"

Provided you have satisfied yourself that mental retardation is not a germane consideration, you may then conclude that he/she is either (1) crazy, or (2) malicious.

If you conclude that your mate is malicious—that the method of his/her behavior is calculated to make you angry or hurt, or to get even or otherwise detract from your pleasure and give you pain—you may stop thinking at that point, content with that explanation. If you conclude that "he/she acts that way because he/she is crazy," it follows that, "When he/she gets better, he/she won't act that way." So you will send him or her to a "getting better" place. Often the first rewards of this attempt is the discovery that you have overturned a whole can of worms you didn't realize was there.

One of the most elemental discoveries of psychodynamic psychiatry is that the signs and symptoms of illness we can perceive in others (i.e., jealousy, rage, withdrawal, etc.) are primarily their attempts at solutions to problems more serious than those problems which they produce.

Going back to our paranoid Cleopatra, suppose that in the real world she is living in a moral igloo of Protestant fundamentalism and faces an unplanned pregnancy by a faithless lover. Certainly passing the late afternoon on Cleopatra's barge is a more comfortable place to be and—voila!—she puts herself there. Surely she is also causing trouble with her insistence on this illogical argument, but by some as yet unfathomed psychical economics, her inner trouble is now less than before. And on this mathematics does the whole system turn: Namely, *how to make life less painful—hopefully without resorting to craziness.*

Now return to our doubting housewife (or husband) and consider that were her mate or anyone else able to make the equation of pain and pleasure work more favorably for her, then she might stop her unrealistic but logically quite easily understood behavior. From where does her pain stem? It could come from anywhere in the infinite complexity that human creativity can construct. Possibly the source is the reality of her own unattractiveness; or sexually mixed feelings (perhaps it is she who is curious about being with other women rather than her husband).

Question: How often do you, in relating to others, protest that they're crazy? Perhaps it is time to pause and reflect that "craziness" is more often "canniness" when seen from its underside.

2

Who Do You Think You Are, Anyway?

"Follow not me and my ideas and my insight into you, but follow you. Cease letting your existence be a thoughtless accident.

—*Karl Jaspers*

In order to understand somebody else for a change or otherwise, we find ourselves attempting to understand the belief or premise that underlies their feeling or behavior. Once persuaded that a human act is not a reflex such as the blinking of an eye or the jerking of a knee or salivating in the presence of tempting food, we are then ready to look to the higher centers where such factors as thinking, feeling, belief and memory are considered to reside (albeit in a mysterious relationship to cerebral cell structure).

We shall by-pass the so-called conditioned reflex wherein these factors of memory and feeling, etc. become fixed to acts with minimal conscious awareness, such that people appear reflexic when in fact memory and feeling are inherently present. What we will do is examine belief as a representative cerebral phenomenon to explain the behavior of others.

Manifest and Latent Behavior and Beliefs

To begin, let's become more conversant with the terms "manifest" and "latent" as they relate to behavior and belief, for we shall use them frequently throughout the book. "Manifest" refers to actions whose motive is immediately apparent—such as the action of quickly removing one's hand from a flame. "Latent" motives, on the other hand, are apparent only through inference.

At a gut level we are frequently aware that some act or comment is not what it appears to be—does not mean what it manifestly says. The query, "I wonder what he meant by that?" or the comment, "I don't think he really meant that," seem to naturally follow such events. What we are saying is, "It doesn't match: I experience the event dysynchronously." There is a double message, as opposed to a gut reaction of acceptance and belief when some act comes across as true. Perhaps we may have to consider a new definition of truth in the interpersonal

15

sphere by saying that a true interpersonal happening is when manifest and underlying or latent content are synchronously one.

However, there is also a lurking danger toward an overinvestment in such a search for underlying or latent content. For no one wants to be too energetically challenged to look at all of his behavior for its possible underlying causes, especially if the act is manifestly kind and/or beneficent.

A simple rule would be, leave all kind and giving behavior free of digging investigation for there appears to be enough of the opposite kind of behavior to devote one's analytic time to. An exception, of course, would be attempts at conscious manipulation, wherein someone treats you kindly and generously but you know it as out of character and so you may wonder what guilt feeling is causing him to act so nicely.

Returning now to the point: disharmony between manifest appearance and what is latent or underlying is a major cause of interpersonal tension. A few examples of remarks which reflect such feeling are "I knew something was wrong the minute you came in," or "Okay, what's the matter now," or "All right, are we in for another day of that ...?"

What the observer is saying is simply this: "I know that when you appear like 'A' you will subsequently act like 'B.'" Hearing this is often all the other needs to promptly proceed to the "B" performance, accusing the observer of seduction in the process.

What can we do about it? Well, let's try to figure it out together in this chapter. Let's try to figure out how underlying beliefs, feelings or ideas affect our behavior.

How We View Others

One set of beliefs which plays a predominant part in determining how we fare with others is our judgment on the issue of whether they are possessions of ours, have a role to play or are free. Throughout our text we shall be referring to these beliefs as *View #1*, *View #2* and *View #3*.

View #1 people may be heard to say:

-You belong to me and must do my bidding ... I don't belong to you! (Sometimes said as, "You're married to me but I'm single.")

-Stop disobeying—regardless of what I do or don't do to you.

-You're obviously very confused or else just plain ornery ... and if you don't shape up, I'll have to either punish you or trade you for a better model.

-What do you mean you don't feel like making love tonight? (You are my possession and must obey my commands.)

View #2 people protest:

-Tit for tat. You do your part or I won't do mine.

-Unless you fulfill your role obligations you forfeit any compassion I may feel for you.

-Good bargaining potential here: I'll agree to your terms on the condition that you agree with mine.

-Of course you can't do that—it interferes with services you owe me.

-Look, don't give me that headache routine again. It's Friday night! I've worked hard all week and have it coming!

Whereas *View #3* people simply say:

-I don't recognize your right to prevent my fulfillment for your own selfish ends. I recognize and accept as valid only part of your anticipations from me.

-Beyond that, your anticipations are not acceptable because they prevent me from fulfilling my own needs. Let us reason together and discover if we can be mutually supportive and life fulfilling.

-You have as much right to your health and happiness as I, and my needs from you are no more important than your needs from me.

Let's consider an imaginary dialogue between mates of the different views:

View #1 Mate speaking: What do you mean you don't feel like making love tonight? (You are my possession.)

View #2 Mate replies: But, Darling, don't you understand that I just can't perform on request? Maybe if we went out to dinner first or shared some wine and conversation (if you played the role of lover).

Continuing View #1 Mate: Look, don't give me that "headache" routine again, it's Friday night. I've worked hard all week and I have it coming (that's your role).

Recognize the pattern? But the conversation would go differently if the View #1 husband had a *View #3* wife.

View #3 Mate replies: So, it's Friday, who cares? I've had a hard day and all I want to do is get some sleep. Just knock it off (I am my own woman).

And obviously if that View #3 wife had been approached by a View #3 husband, the conversation might have gone like this:

View #3 Mate: Darling, I'm so horny I'm going up the wall. What do you say?

View #3 Mate replying: Sweetheart, I'll try, but no promises; it's been one hell of a day.

"It is one thing to be the same substance; another to be the same man; and, a third to be the same person."

—John Locke

How We Present Ourselves to Others

Another set of beliefs we enjoy is that we are experienced as we present our-selves … and that we present ourselves as we are.

In true fact, there are substantial differences between our real selves, the selves we present and the ways in which we are experienced by others:

The *Real* me:	*The Me I Hold Myself Up to Be*	*The Me Experienced by Others*
my true acts	my image of me	the me you judge and evaluate
ideas	the me I present	the me upon whom you project
feelings	and expect/demand	your wishes and expectations
attitudes	others to see	
	my view of me	
views		
my real body	my presumptions	the potential me
my performance	ideals	the me whom you view

The following drawings give a visual illustration of all the possible combinations.

The Real Me

The Real You

The Real Me

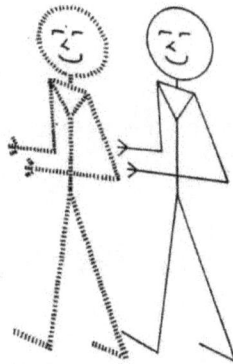

The You You Hold
Yourself Up To Be

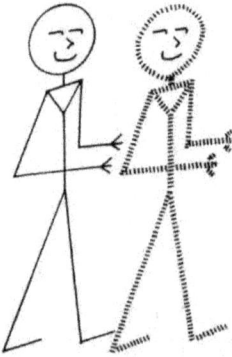

The Me I Hold
Myself Up To Be

The Real You

The Me I Hold
Myself Up To Be

The You You Hold
Yourself Up To Be

The Me I Hold
Myself Up To Be

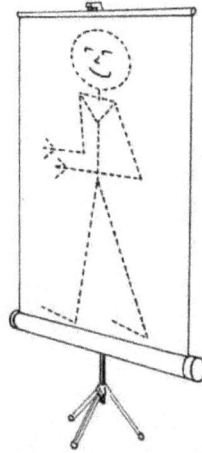

The You I Experience

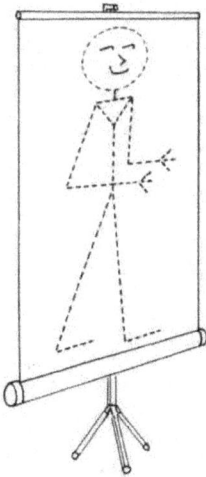

The Me You Experience

The Real You

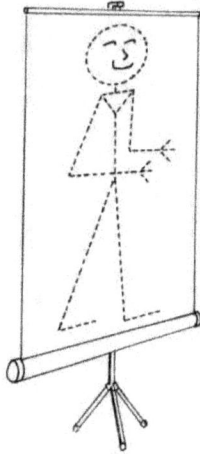

The Me You Experience

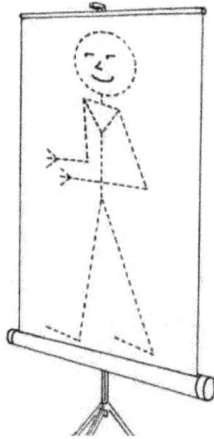

The You You Hold
Yourself Up To Be

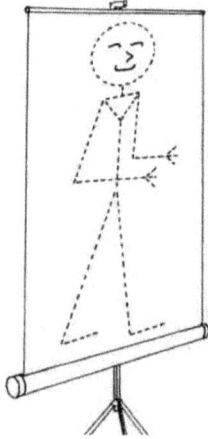

The Me You Experience

The You I Experience

The You I Experience   Can =   The You You Hold Yourself Up To Be   Can =   The Real You

The Real Me   Can =   The Me I Hold Myself Up To Be   Can =   The Me You Experience

Throughout our text we shall observe people from these three basic postures (the real me, the me I present and the me you see and vice versa) as they attempt to interrelate.

We shall see how people's unconscious elemental views of each other (View #1: you are my possession; View #2: we are role related; View #3: you are a free and equal person who must fulfill your own needs no matter how they affect my wishes and anticipations from you.) muddy the waters of communication and lead to misunderstandings and pain.

The interpersonal experience is, at the barest minimum, quite complicated. It behooves us all to become skilled players of the interpersonal space.

To accomplish intimacy you and I must together achieve the DUAL mode, in which each participant is simultaneously the real self, the self that is presented and the self that is experienced—and that self must view the other as free and equal, rather than bound by the needs we project onto him or her.

Projected upon these world spaces is a concept of time which goes forward and backward from the present in the following fashion: An immediate past history which is the territory of remorse, immediate past history which is the territory of regret, and a remote past history which may be considered the territory of the obsolete as well as an immediate future of expectation, immediate future of wish and a remote future of prayer.

The point of Chapter 3 is that there are no such things as persons; only our opinions about what a person is.

So—in order to understand someone else we've got to begin by understanding our own ideas, beliefs and feelings about how others have become the persons they "are," i.e., how they have developed minds from their brains and personalities from their bodies—as well as how so they sojourn in their unique places at their special times.

3

The Idea of a Person—What Is a Person?

*"One's description of the other as organism is as different as
one's description of him as person; as is the side of the vase
from the profile of a face in the classic Gestalt figure."*

—R. D. Laing

"Mind," "time" and "persons" are only concepts. There are no such objects as mind, time or persons. And whereas there may be places without bodies in them, there never has been a body that wasn't in a place.

Since there never was a body that wasn't in a place, it is silly to think of talking about bodies except in the places that these bodies are. All bodies are absolutely and categorically connected to their places. So instead of thinking about bodies we really ought to think in terms of a new word of ourselves and others. Each of us is a body/place.

Now, our ideas about the continuity of those bodies in those places with: (1) their necessary and essential properties; (2) the notions of how those bodies become persons with minds; and (3) are responsible for their subsequent behavior, are crucial to any understanding of others. We may profess to have this understanding, yet few of us are ever called upon to articulate our beliefs on this in a formal fashion.

There are, however, such things as other bodies. So let's talk a little bit about bodies.

Bodies are composed of cells, tissues and organ systems, and support the life of persons. But there is no such thing as life and there is no such thing as a person so already we are into a complicated communication.

Bodies *are*. But as soon as we say *alive*, we are into an idea of life. So the interface between objects and ideas is very complicated. Let us say for the moment that there are cells, tissues and organ systems plus a unique central nervous system in the bodies of persons. These cells, etc. bring the world to them (to those bodies) via processes called tasting, smelling, feeling, looking, hearing and touching. This data is organized (that's another concept)—experienced (that's another concept, it's not a chemical reaction)—through processes called remembering,

25

learning and reasoning. We symbolize into language the concepts of time, life, mind, death, identity, God, morality and persons. Somehow at the bottom of every discussion of what a person is, there is always that so-called magnificent leap from the flesh to the person and, though our brains cannot fathom it, we must remain mindful of the presence and the mystery of how bodies become persons and how brains become minds.

Whatever persons are, they are of their bodies, in their places, and at their times.

The time that it is on the clock may or may not be the time in which the person you are trying to understand is living.

For me, it's 1:00 o'clock Thursday afternoon, January 1978. What time is it for you? You may be in a nostalgic mood, thinking and feeling as if it were 5 or 6 chronological years ago, and having a delayed grief reaction to the death of your beloved mother who died one year ago today. So suddenly, we are in two different time zones. You are in a zone of grief or remorse or remembering whereas the clock and I agree that it is 1:00 o'clock Thursday afternoon, January 1978. Your existence may be remote from that time. If we want to understand others we have to also know what time it is with them.

We also have to know where they are, not merely in terms of being in downtown Pinellas, but also whether or not they are walking home from being fired from their job; having just been in a terrible automobile accident; in the process of changing religions; discouraged and disappointed in their children; and so forth.

Place can be external, like Pinellas County, or it can be internal like doubting; fearing; changing convictions; going through mid-life crises, divorce, separation; being in love or out of love.

Thus we note that these are the bodies in which people live and are. We observe time frames and zones in which people can be discovered to be quite independent of clock times. We note external places that bodies and so-called persons may be described as being in. Then we have another phenomenon, called the interpersonal space or place, which may be a sub-category of the place/ notions already mentioned, but it is important that we give it a separate localization.

As we wrote in Chapter 2 in the interpersonal sphere there are three major identifications that persons have. They can be "the real they"—which means the "they" that has been consensually validated and which is validated and which is reflected in their history of being and performance. They can be the "they that they hold themselves up to be"—the facade, the act, the game, the sham. And they can be the "they" that you experience. And these can be compartmentalized into these subcategories of experiencing other people: (1) as your possession, (2) as role responsible and (3) as free. Likewise you can be the "real you," the "you you hold yourself up to be" or the "you that they experience." That provides the various modes of interacting for any given moment when you are with someone that you are trying to understand. If you don't know which of those modes of interaction you are each in, communications between you can get very confusing.

And if you have no agreement as to which of those modes you are in, you can get into even more trouble.

We suggest that the only mode of interacting which allows for something called intimacy is the mode where I am experienced by you as free and autonomous and you are experienced by me as free and autonomous, and we are both coincidentally our real selves and the selves we hold ourselves up to be.

How to facilitate this process will be the essential task of our text.

4

Your Place or Mine?

"Being is what remains after analysis."

—*Marcel*

While counseling a married couple recently, I observed that the husband felt so out of place at his job and in the community where they lived that his "place-lessness" (or place-conflicted life) rendered his existence inoperative. Thus it was an unattainable ambition for him to secure a workable interpersonal relationship with his wife, who also lived there.

In understanding others we must be mindful that people who are out of communion with the place in which they find themselves are not good candidates for an interpersonal relationship. Furthermore, "place" is a much broader concept than geography and is not construed merely in terms of house, city and state, but in terms of one's overall cultural place, which comprehends one's ethic; one's view of the world; one's philosophy; one's sense of interpersonal and friendship relationships; one's inner sense of destiny; one's notions of personal place in the cosmos; and role in government; ideas of love, justice, etc.—one's compatibility with one's flesh; one's sense of the nature of cause-and-effect in his behavior; one's understanding of how to separate from responsibility one's notion of his essential and marginal properties; one's sense of personal continuity through time. These are not topics for graduate courses at an ivy league college, but are, in fact, the rightful and proper business of *all* individuals who genuinely want to secure satisfactory relationships with searching others.

Thus, while we may seldom be challenged to formally articulate our philosophy in the earlier hours of encounter, the longer we put off an honest exposure of our values the less likely we are to have successful unions.

A devastated young coed at the Rhode Island School of Design found out the afternoon of her marriage dress rehearsal that her spouse-to-be objected to one of the black bridesmaids. Her tearful reprise was, "Could I ever be happy with someone who was in that place?"

While "Who are you?" seems to have been the question that most of us asked in getting to know our new-found loves, another question would now appear to be more productive: "*Where* are you?" In this way we can soften the confrontation and at the same time collect crucial data for our judgments.

Prince Charles recently identified his criteria for a spouse he might select for the role of next Queen of England, by saying that she should be someone who was accustomed to living in a manor house. We can appreciate the candidness of such a statement, for a person who knew about those places—had been to those places where it was likely that a queen would be and whose performance in those places could be identified, inspected and judged—would in fact be a more likely candidate for a successful queen than someone with no prior experience in those same places.

We can ask questions about moral places where one has been and moral decisions that one has made to determine the qualifications another has for an important relationship.

There is no greater lament than that of the spouse, lover, mistress—whomever—who cries that his partner has been unjust and has betrayed him. Reviewing the dreadful literature on family homicide and exploring the rationale behind such heinous retaliation, the argument often is that the retaliation was based on "righting the moral injustice" of the violator (the murdered) of the code of ethics held by the murderer. The idea of others not knowing their place and invading ours seduces us to our most primitive responses of self-defense.

In attempting to define the time and value spaces of those with whom we interact and to join them and truly be with them there, instead of merely, it is necessary to humble ourselves with the knowledge that no datum can ever be properly and fully separated from the placement and efficiency of the observer. Then realize that in the study of another, we and our placement are crucial variables.

In understanding others, the instrument of self and our perceptive lenses must be as free from the distortion of prejudgment as possible. Once so placed we are less likely to see others as objects or unsurely perceive their acts and are more likely to see people as moored to their cultural and biological pasts, and as promised to contracts and agreements for which none of the small print was legible at the time of signature and now being too frightened to move.

I recall an occasion in my practice when an unshaven, simple, but extremely successful businessman admonished me, following a visit by his chic and well-coiffed nouveau riche wife, to tell her that for him to give up his (so termed by her) "idiosyncrasies" was a far graver enterprise than her simplistic formulation allowed. He had some profound sense about which combination of his traits were likely to bond and thus jointly depart in the transition. His point was simply this: in requesting the diminution of one trait, she may not have bargained for the possibility of its taking with it several others. Her sense of the relationship of his parts to his whole was too simplistic. She didn't know that giving up what appeared to her to be relatively minor traits was for him like moving from Milwaukee to Key West. To extend our perspective from the vision of a simple act to its place in the fabric of the other's world place is a most provocative and sobering experience.

Another patient of mine, an independent career journalist and mother of one son, recounted this story of a trysting weekend at a Cape Cod resort. When her lover judged that the flowers on her bathing cap were gaudy and "not her" she became more miffed by the remark than was her usual style. He persisted in his position, now furthering the affront by peeling them off while she left on a brief errand. Upon her return she dissolved, first into tears and then fury at this invasion of her territory, which he still considered a minor insult and presumption.

What happened here is repeated thousands of times in the skirmishes and full battles between spouses, lovers and friends. A misunderstanding of how far we may move into another's space without trespassing ... a misunderstanding of how important things are to the significant others in our lives ... is serious business, and how wise we are in recognizing this is a vital skill which this book hopes to sharpen. For these seemingly petty misunderstandings have a profound theme, and that is this:

When invited into another person's space, it is crucial to comprehend the vast complexity of the experience. It is not necessary that we undertake a philosophical inquiry as to what their views of God, genetics, time, space, and ethics are, but we must recognize that we join others *at our peril* unless we are prepared to appreciate that only when we become synchronized by empathy are we likely to both be at the same place at the same time.

"When I asked you into 'x' I hardly meant that you could do 'y.'"

The "x–y" contracts have been known to be extremely stark and even crazy. However, it surely behooves one to press on for a more in-depth understanding of what may rightfully follow from permission to enter or join another person's place. Assumptions, presumptions, intuition and logic are often inappropriate guideposts for such a process: "Yes, you may make love to me but you'll have to use the children's bathroom."

Much more can be said about knowing or intuiting the qualifiers attendant to our primary agreements, and surely it doesn't take much experience in the interpersonal space to appreciate that logic should not be your only guide or friend.

In our next chapter we shall formalize some of these arguments into a comprehensive body/mind/place model for persons.

5

A Mind/Body/Place Model for Persons

"I will not harken not to know the whole of me ... I must hear no less."

—Sophocles

For the last several hundred years not feeling or functioning well has been considered proper complaint for the services of men of medicine. Their formula has been to explore the functioning of body organs and to provide remedy to them when they are noted to be ill performing or broken.

Thus far in our text we have repudiated that formulation for the "not feeling well" feelings called mental illness. In this chapter we shall directly challenge the role of physician treaters of mental illness as we prepare a new model for a more profound understanding of the "not feeling (or behaving) well" others in our lives and shall construct our mind/body/place model for persons.

Let's begin with these observations:

1.   There is no such thing as "mental health." "Mental" and "health" are only words, and only words which symbolize notions or ideas about how people behave, feel and think.

2.   There are such beings as persons who may not feel or function well.

3.   An extraordinary vocabulary and literature of theory has emerged to account for a condition of not feeling or behaving or thinking well, when no dysfunctional body parts can be found. In faith and allegiance to those explanations of "illness," many troubled "patients" have reasoned themselves into feeling and acting better, facilitated by so-called psychotherapists, psychiatrists and psychoanalysts.

The relationship between feeling better and being healthy is not a simple one in medicine in general. In psychiatry the absence of those key feelings of anxiety or depression has generally come to mean the absence of mental illness.

But *an absence of mental illness is not mental health!* There is a non-ill/non-health space along that hypothesized axis which most investigators believe we travel in going from states of illness to states of health, and that locus in space and

33

time (i.e., not ill and not healthy), is an extremely interesting one to contemplate because it provides a plateau of human existence that is uncluttered with theories and techniques for the treatment of illness, and fertile for notions of the meaning and purpose of one's life. This state is boredom and it deserves a fresh new look.

The ideas and treatments of Freudian psychiatrists and analysts may be relevant for ending inner confusion; depersonalization; conflict and pain; facilitating the end of anxiety and/or depression—but they are inadequate techniques for aiding the journey from non-illness (which is less than health) to self-actualization or health. The non-sick patient, after the transient euphoria of no longer feeling sick, is bored until he has expressed himself somehow other than as one merely without symptoms or signs of illness.

For one who travels this road alone, without the aid of professional helpers, boredom may be the best indicator of having reached a non-ill mental or emotional state. It therefore can be thought of as a victorious state, indicative of having won an inner battle with one's previous "ill" condition.

But though the battle has been won, the war is not yet over. And from here on, winning the war becomes a very subjective battle which has little to do with generalities about state of illness or health.

Abraham Maslow has made some interesting observations on this point. He introduces us to the adjective "fully" with regard to the condition of being human and, as is the case with many Eastern languages, asks us Westerners to appreciate that all adjectives have a "for me-ness" understood about them. For example, when we say this is a beautiful flower we really mean this is a "for me" beautiful flower. He proceeds to show that the understanding of my health is far more challenging than understanding health in the abstract; suggesting that there is a "for me" health which has a unique and special quality, and requires quite different skills to achieve than those used to relieve any patient of his anxiety or depression which may be a quite medically legitimate psychiatric enterprise, saying nothing about the "for me" health.

As Maslow puts it, "Those feeling experiences define who you peculiarly are, how you are, what your potentialities are, what your style is, what your pace is, what your tastes are, where your body is going, where your personal biology is taking you and how you are different and similar to others." He also concludes, "Healthy people are very different in kind and degree from not-sick people."

The point of this is to define that interval state of boredom across which one must transit in the process of going from psychological illness to personal health.

Maslow further allows an alternative for using the classic medical modeling of autopsy to understand sickness and then inferring health as the condition of non-illness. Instead of using asylums and psychiatric wards of general hospitals as our proper laboratories, we are encouraged to study peak experiences and great men. He goes on with Erickson to tell us that trust, autonomy, intimacy, industry and identity do not fall into place when schizophrenia, phobia or psychotic depression fade and resolve … though insight and pharmacotherapy may very well take us to diminished illness or even non-illness, an entirely different process may be required to take us to health. In my judgment no language or theory speaks better to this process, no philosophy more carefully identifies this phenomenon, than existential psychiatry, and no more identifiable state of being characterizes the interspace more effectively than boredom.

Boredom is a primary state of out-of-worldliness. It is echoed in the wail of the wanderer in the territory of the alien and the lost. It is being, without adequate singular, dual or plural relationships; it is beingness without thereness.

Personal health may now be defined as "not bored" for insofar as one is not bored the following characteristics of personal peace and self-fulfillment are realized, namely, "I am not where I should not be" and "I am where I deserve and want to be."

Outsight of other persons in their world places is as worthy of our attention and concern as are body problems or "intrapsychic" problems. The integration of my inner parts may make me an organized whole person (and I am in debt to my early teachers who conveyed that singular focus on the "human condition") but orientation to place is at least as important.

The comparison of insomnia to sleeping lends itself to the relationship of boredom to self-actualization and health. The insomniac is not just a non-sleeper; he is in a pained state. He says, "I should be sleeping; I need my sleep; it is my right to sleep" and in the non-sleep state he is irritable, angry and frightened.

Psychological theorists insist that understanding minds is essential to understanding persons, and that a proper understanding of the mind/body relationship clarifies how "mind health" leads to better body functioning and normal behavior. We insist that scientifically exact probing into person/place dynamics helps our understanding of normal healthy personal behavior.

We need to make a more careful exploration of individuals in stress situation places as opposed to individuals reacting to stress situations. There are no such things as stresses over there and people over here who meet them as if on a battlefield. People are in stress and cannot ever be understood as other than *of* the stress and intimate with the situation which troubles them. The stresses of our world are not remote. They are here and we are in and of them. We do not react except metaphorically to a stress. One is present in stress, and must be accounted for.

In contrast to the nebulous notions of minds in bodies it is helpful to talk more concretely and exactly about persons in places. Instead of medicalizing our human condition (as Ivan Illich so harshly pointed out in his recent text of protest, *Medical Nemesis*), we should realize that "The widest polarities in therapy lie in whether the doctor turns to what can be discovered by science—that is biological events (and I would like to add psychological events)—or whether he turns to the freedom of man," and if you know Jaspers's work well enough you will understand that "freedom" is in fact an existential notion of *choice* of *place* and the constructing of a *life through decisions*. He goes on to say, "Life I can treat but to freedom I can only appeal."

Appealing to freedom begins in a very real way with knowing where individuals live. Thus, in answer to the query of our prior chapter, "Your place or mine?," we must always try to reply, "Ours, with as much of me as I can bear to deliver!" For there are really no such things as minds—no such things as personalities—no such forces as *destrado* or libido. We must refocus upon the human condition by noting that *whereas there may be places without people, there has never been a person who was not in a place* and then asserting that *his actual relationships to his actual place is at least as interesting as his hypothesized mind is to his actual body.*

Since all persons are necessarily in and of places, a more global concept for understanding man would be one of person/place rather than one which allows and encourages the fractioning of a whole person to thing and theory parts. Understanding personal as opposed to body health demands an appreciation of this fact—for bodies are of their parts, but persons are of the world.

Outsight or world view is a worthy rival for insight in understanding the human condition. Man in "his" space, world, nature and family is not separate from them. Liberty from such figure/ground would be as ridiculous for self meaning as talking about the individual liberty of our fingers shorn loose from our hands. The notion of man's intimacy with space and place is as crucial a topic for the contemplation of psychologists and psychiatrists as is man's relationship to his body, and just because physicians have a monopoly on the latter, their models may not be as useful in the former categories.

However fascinating it may be at the anatomy, autopsy or operating table to see how the "thing" parts of people affected their behavior and health, there is far greater exhilaration in the quest for understanding the phenomena of *people in places* and *time*. It involves, of course, giving up the myth of finding the missing enzyme to sponge up the psychoanalytic theories. Nicholas Hobbes said it when he wrote: "A therapy aimed at uncovering repression cannot be expected to bend for adaptation to a patient confronted with the unrelenting clear awareness of the absurd and desperate condition of the world in which he lives."

Psychiatrists have paid too much attention to the deviations of patients from "our" places and not enough to their "private" worlds. So let's see how to find out about our patients' private worlds. With Becket, Camus, Kafka, Nietzsche, Kierkegaard, Buber, Heidegger, Husserl and Strauss, let's try to learn the existential vocabulary so that we can think more extensively about man in his world.

With these concepts we are inquiring into people's overall world existence and striving for a way of sojourning into their spaces and unique times of their lives. With such a vocabulary, patients and friends avoid being comprehended with the same language which describes the flow of liquids or the color of chairs. Let's try to diagram this and then in the coming chapters we shall refer to our model.

Of Their Bodies

In Their Other People Places

Whose cells, tissues and organ systems support their life and whose unique central nervous system brings the world to them via tasting, smelling, feeling, looking, hearing and touching, and organizes this data via processes called "remembering," "learning," "reasoning," "symbolizing into language," and "creating" concepts of time, life, mind, death, identity, duty, God, morality, persons, beauty and love.

The Idea of Persons Having Been

Evolution, Culture, Anthroplogy, Parents, Genetics

Now have their essential and necessary properties and are always
    of their bodies
    in their places
    at their times

make choices, adapt, act, adjust, speak, avoid pain, seek pleasure, repeat old ways, survive

become unto their death

Where they react with others in the nine modes identified in Chapter 2.

1. the real me	1. the real you
2. the me I hold myself up to be	2. the you you hold yourself up to be
3. the me you experience	3. the you experience
as possession	as possession
as role responsible	as role responsible
as free	as free

At Their Time

1. The remote past-zone of the obsolete.
2. The immediate past-zone of regret.
3. The immediate past-zone of remorse.
4. The present-zone of now.
5. The immediate future-zone of wish.
6. The mediate future-zone of wish.
7. The remote future-zone of prayer.

In Their And Idea Places

1. Inner zone of personal values, ideas, beliefs, attitudes, judgments, prejudgments, hopes and aspirations.
2. External zone—their oriented place of objects and facts where the laws of nature, i.e., physics and chemistry, prevail.

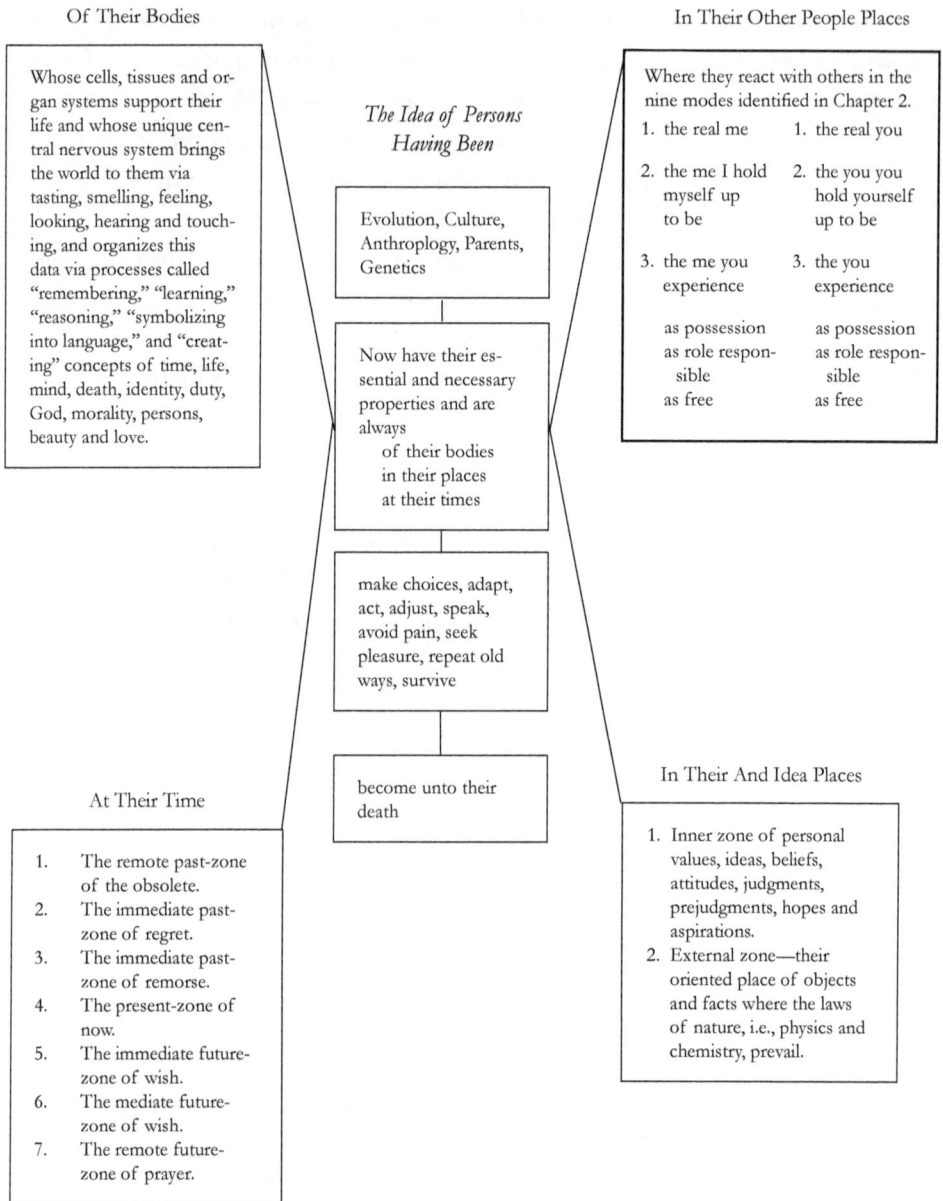

Most modes are plural or anonymous because the participants are either (a) not presenting their real selves to the other or (b) not experiencing the other as free.

Only in the dual mode—where (1), (2) and (3) are synonymous and each is experiencing the other as free—can intimacy be achieved.

6

Gathering a Psychobiography

"The only reality of our past is how we experience it in the present, thus, phenomenologic time has nothing to do with clock time and every generation begins at the beginning."

—Karl Jaspers

What's Identity?

The importance of a process called identification has been amply discussed in the psychoanalytic and sociological literature to account for the fact that Japanese people raise Japanese children and American middle-class Long Island Jewish mothers raised their particular brand of young sons and daughters.

This chapter shall consider individual identification. One of the primary requirements for a personal and separate identification is cleavage from the parent with "clean edges." One cannot have his identification if he is merely an appendage of another.

Surely we have seen in our own lives many whose identifications are marred by residual clinging to their parents or parental surrogates and who, in very real ways, endure as extensions of others. The likelihood of severe mental illness in the non-separated person is much greater than in those more individuated.

Poem:
syd at the drugstore[3]
nurture abhors a vacuum
and all the bulls of high resolve
cannot replace the
dove of touching
the lamb of sweet familiar breath
you cannot become a not someone
you can only be
like uncle ed
or miss ester
or syd at the drugstore

---

3   Collected Poems, A. E. Fireman

39

What this poem tries to convey is that in becoming one, separate from the rearing others, one must fix on a real other person. The magnetism of noxious but present others is interesting to pause and reflect upon. Many psychiatric patients come to the awareness that they have become just like another whom they vowed they would not mime. But it isn't possible to be a not-someone. We can only be a someone and, like imprinting in birds, the ones who are there are the ones who convey our name.

We have seen hundreds of instances where children have made high resolves to identify not with the punitive or disappointing parent but with their concept of the opposite of such a person ... only to find to their travail in later life that nature would not allow an identification with an imagined person. One can only be like an other—one cannot grow up to be a non-other.

It is this knowledge that generated a belief in the wisdom of getting to know your girlfriend's mother or boyfriend's father, for there but for the grace of special intervening others goes he/she. When we discern that a special other is like one of his or her parents it is important to tease the likeness apart to know whether they are separate and like, or extensions of the parent. The maneuvers of dealing with the very distinctive differences in these special others about us are formidable.

In understanding somebody else for a change, the concept of whence came they to this place (i.e., what nature and nurturing factors contributed to their present experience) is, of course, crucial.

In the rest of the animal kingdom mothers breed, carry, deliver and rear their offspring with a manner and method indelibly etched into their protoplasm and with a timeless consistency and conformity. This natural way was presumed (it seems to me illogically) to apply to humans as well and consequently a science of child-rearing was long delayed in the evolution of man's knowledge. A real perception of the infant and child as a multi-potential individual rather than an embryonic mass, fully labeled and predestined toward its adult form, was deeply imbedded in the medical literature. The concept of the homunculus[4] gives dramatic evidence of this. The forces that took the fetus through gestation to full intra-uterine maturity and which were later manifested in the growing infant and child were felt to reside intracellularly, and man's nurturing tasks were considered to be reciprocally natural and intuitive. So, it appeared that if the nutriment and

---

4   A tiny or undersized man; a dwarf.

warmth necessary for the sustenance of the biological infant were provided, each child would eventually achieve physical and personal maturity. The hypothesis seems to have been that any woman capable of conceiving was also capable of rearing, and that the essential skills would be as naturally forthcoming as the biological ability to bear children.

The fact of the matter is that the rearing of children is an infinitely complicated, tremendously challenging and gravely important process. Such rearing practices which denied the maturation of personality as a separate phenomenon to biological development are presently considered to have wrought great personal and social ruin.

Every medical student is urged by his teachers to listen to and watch his patients with meticulous care and attention in physical diagnosis. It is a paradoxical fact that the beat of the heart; the rate of the pulse; the frequency of the respirations; the location and distribution of zones of body tenderness; gait; stance; etc., were examined by men of medicine in exquisite detail, while the verbal productions of the neurotic and psychotic patients were dismissed by medical specialists as idle chatter, ramblings of mania or sheer nonsense. So, also manifest dream contents, the details of his phobias and compulsions and unusual verbal associative patterns to hysterical symptoms were likewise never examined with the same medical scrutiny as were a patient's physical dimensions.

These matters never received their rightful attention until the investigations of Sigmund Freud. Freud's genius was his dedication to the facts of life, free of the prejudices of past intellectual history and present civilized judgments. Freud looked at human behavior more objectively than any investigator prior to him had ever consistently done. "Consistent" is very important here, for the argument of his originality does not hold up as well as the argument for his brilliant perseverance. Although Freud did break new ground in many areas, he was unquestionably the messenger of history—on the one hand carrying the torch of insight lit by other investigators to new heights and again kindling new theories along the path. Just as he had the patience and curiosity to attend to such verbal productions, so did he have the wisdom to look at children.

First, he looked at them through the recollections of his disturbed adults, but often in letters to close friends he exhorted young investigators to attend to the productions and behavior of children in vivo.

Here, he believed, was a profound new source of psychiatric information. His forever famous essays, *Three Contributions of the Theory of Sexuality*, for the first time called the scientists of the world to consider the concept of infantile sexuality. The word sexuality was an unfortunate historical choice. It immediately discouraged the prudent readership of the early 20th Century and exposed his writings to a smear of prejudice which still is not completely washed away. Freud had the incisive perception to observe that sexuality is not a phenomenon of *deus ex machina* that appears from behind the chorus of pre-adolescence, full-formed and ready to articulate its timeless message … far to the contrary, he taught that sexuality had a beginning, a course, a fulfillment, a maturation and a senescence. He saw suckling, fondling, child play, bowel, bladder and auto-genital experiences, as early manifestations of the final sexuality which permits and enhances the heterosexual love relationship of adults. And he had the audacity to proclaim his observations.

A result of these provocative observations was the further realization that the child grew and matured with a direction marked by definite milestones—the so-called oral, anal and genital states of development—and that coincident with these were collateral events in the family and society, and that these interactional experiences etched a prognosis into the life plan of each individual to be erased only with severe adult effort and anguish.

For most of us it would be hard to strip away from our thinking and distill from our rearing experiences the sources for our selection of a love partner, and to scrutinize the process with scientific objectivity. Yet, the fact of the matter is that in his perceptive paper *Instincts and their Vicissitudes*, Freud was the first to clarify that instincts had aims and objects which were functions of the rearing experiences rather than of one's biological endowment.

The only biological endowment that Freud or contemporary authors have been able to scientifically validate as omnipresent in the growing life were the primary love (or coming together) and the aggressive (or survival) instincts. Who was to be loved and who to be hated, or how this love was to be effected and what was to be the modality for expressing this hate—these remained for the rearing experience to define.

In my own life, I had the great good fortune to have been raised not only by my parents but by my mother's parents as well, though not in the same house.

My grandparents' home was only a few blocks away and this allowed me a sense of separate place as well as of surrogate parents. My mother was a quick, witty, attractive, domineering, anxious and outspoken woman. My father, on the other hand, was passive, apologetic, not wanting to make a fuss, slow to anger and probably the most generous person I have ever met. My grandmother was as gentle, warm and accommodating as my prepubescent mind could conceive while my grandfather was brilliant, powerful, wise, aloof and the boss of them all. How exciting to have had such a variegated input so that my manhood could include the ways of a patriarch with the capitulations of a "Let's make it nice and don't aggravate your mother" father, while hoping someday to marry a mix of their respective wives!

Now, returning to our text—

In interacting with another and in attempting to discern what he is about, we must understand not only with whom he is primarily identified but also what *ideals* of those others he has incorporated into his own existence as goals or, to use the analysts' vocabulary "What are his superego ideals?" What must he *be*, what must he *do* in order to be *his* ideal self and how energized is this inclination? We ask this latter question so we may understand how shamed and guilty he will feel if he fails.

A tragic occurrence is often seen in instances where parental messages have been misperceived and sons and daughters have taken mistaken clues to mean one goal when another less formidable one would have been quite acceptable.

Thus a primary question in all interpersonal interactions is "Who else lives up there with you in that magical place where you have sojourned from flesh to mind, from body to person? Who are the special and myriad others to whom you must pay dues and account for your behavior else you blame me or engulf me in your guilt if I become an unwitting accomplice to your behavior?"

In assessing the dynamics of crimes of violence these points are often dramatically revealed, wherein unknowing partners of these criminals participate in sexual activities with them—not knowing that below the lust and pleasure there lurks harsh punitive devils.

Discovering a Psychobiography

*"What opportunities we let pass lacking in the
simple virtue of full human presence."*

—*Karl Jaspers*

During my earliest training years at the Boston V.A. Hospital, I had the good fortune to inherit an exceptionally well-funded program which offered hospitality to expatriated European physicians.

Among those at this particular hospital were several Viennese psychiatrists whose cultural history was such that they had never seen the likes of our American veterans from Oregon or Georgia.

Their terse apprehensive utterances of "Yeaah-ah" and "Meybe" very often elicited diagnoses of simple schizophrenia and schizoid personality—when the truth was merely that "That's just the way folks are in Portland."

Pushing psychiatric diagnoses across cultural lines has always been of dubious utility. The charade of West German psychological formulations for South African mental aberrations provides a preposterous analogy.

There are profound cultural differences not only among those raised in different countries but even those raised in the same family.

Whereas sociologists and anthropologists have used *culture* to speak for the characteristics of aggregates of people, we offer a formulation of *individual culture* and argue that insofar as we fail to comprehend the *unique* culture of the special people in our lives, we are limited to a marginal and poor interpersonal relationship with them and will likely forfeit the joys of encounter. The customed ways of our individual mothers, absent/present fathers and siblings in their special neighborhoods, embroiled in their private agonies and ecstasies, demand that in our relationship to others we begin with this cardinal premise: "*He is other than I!*"

And, before we share one moment of personal intercourse, this one thing is certain: *he knows me not, nor I him.*

My gift may not pleasure him. My needs may not be his concern. My satisfaction is not his responsibility.

Well, before we presume to exercise our demands, we must likewise appreciate a second truth: the *quality of their response must only be measured against their essential resources, not against our needs!*

I am reminded here of that superb British movie about a soccer player whose mistress was finally tormented to suicide by his critical comparison between what she provided in terms of his needs as opposed to her capability. The command of God to be charitable is noted by the Jewish rabbis to be measured not by *amount* given but by its *percentage* of assets. Knowledge of another's capacities to give can well begin with an awareness of their formative past.

To say that in order to understand someone else for a change we need to understand how that other resolved Oedipus or Electra situations sounds tantamount to writing a textbook of brain surgery for beauticians. But in more elementary forms it is really a quite feasible enterprise for any caring observer. All it means is that we have to know how someone was raised; grew up; was supported; challenged, threatened, taken through the crucial states of anonymity and object-hood into personhood; how they secured their survival techniques for living as adult members of the human species. These form an excellent beginning for understanding someone else. It is the message of this text that a psychobiography of everyone whom we have the remotest notion of having a satisfactory relation-ship with is surely as worthwhile a task as studying the life of Woodrow Wilson or Bette Davis. I am convinced that many of us are more able to cite the details of growth, development, likes, failures and idiosyncrasies of certain celebrities than we are about our own father, mother, spouse or brother-in-law.

In the practice of psychiatry it is always impressive to see the excitement of discovery that envelopes patients once their curiosity is whet and they are then able to secure (through conversations with siblings, parents, cousins, neighbors etc.), vignettes, anecdotes and missing material for the large blanks and blocks in memory of their formative years. Those mechanisms of suppression, repres-sion, blocking, denial and avoidance are extremely interesting, for they reveal not genetic inclinations of the human personality but the great reluctance of rearing parents and elders to enrich the lives of their children with a more honest and open discussion of the real facts of their family life.

We have misrepresented the facts of life when we naively limit them to tell-ing our children where babies come from. The facts of life which most children crave, those facts of life which will be most helpful to the formation of intact adult personalities (View #3) are the facts of the *true feelings and ideas* which existed in our rearing households.

We hardly suggest that mothers share with their daughters the so-called pri-vate happenings of the bedroom or that fathers discuss with their sons the com-plete details of their businesses. What we do suggest, however, is that the *quality* of life in a family—the frustrations, disappointments, angers, hopes and aspira-tions; the full range of human experiences witnessed by the child—be given vali-dation so that the child's intuition and reality-testing perceptions can be matched to the truths of interpersonal family life, rather than remain facade and charade. The new aphorism would thence be "Spare the truth and distort the child." How-ever, here again we caution you not to misconstrue this to mean that infants and toddlers must now be taken into confidential relationships by parents and older siblings. The art of childrearing should be wed to these directives of being hon-est, truthful and open with children so that what simply emerges is a diminution of the double message. The input of truth must then be scrupulously enhanced as the ears and eyes of the growing child can accommodate the news—I hasten to add, as delivered by caring parents.

How this relates to our enterprise of understanding the other adults in our life is simply this: That *without the experiences of reference for having been understood and having had our interpersonal antenna stimulated by the trust of our parents to tell us the truth, we are less likely to quest for this in our adult lives or know it from role playing even if we found it.* It is solid foundation for the development of a *View #3* approach to life because it builds self-confidence in one's own ability to perceive, analyze and make decisions about reality.

The soul-searching questions to ask yourself at this point are:

"How often do I wonder how another could 'do that *to me?*'"

"How often am I able to detect more subjective motives for their acts?"

"When my response is ambivalent (I can see the logic and acceptable reason behind their acts, yet it continues to deeply trouble me), am I responding in a View #1 or #2 way because of some third-party ghosts I am not conscious of?"

"Do I accept the other person's right to act out of self-interest, where such actions cause me pain? If not, is it because they have no right (in my *View #1*) to personal pleasure or happiness—they should be entirely and solely devoted to me—or because (*View #2*) such acts do not conform to my idea of the acceptable patterns for our relationship?"

Are we *View #1* people protesting:

-Anything you do which causes me discomfort is not allowed.

-No, it has nothing to do with what I do.

-You are purposely ignoring my pleasure by …

Are we *View #2* people stating:

-That is an unforgivable reaction to me, your spouse/parent/friend.

-I'll never give up this habit. It is my sole right.

-Have you no respect for our relationship?

Or are we *View #3* people, asking:

-Did you realize how much that hurt me?

-But do you really enjoy doing that for me—we could hire it done or share the task.

-Okay, here are all the chores we mutually agree must be done for our mutual satisfaction. Which do you want to do, and which do I agree to do?

7

The Diamond Rule of Living

"We cannot even see a truth until we have a commitment to it."

—*Kierkegaard*

One of life's most established ethical principles, embodied in the Golden Rule, needs revision if it is to be applied universally to all human interactions. In the admonishment, "Do unto others as you would be done by them," there is really no provision for unique and individual patterns of behavior. Can you imagine for example a "Golden Rule" defense for a person who has been charged with the crime of having done to another exactly as he would have liked to be done to the other, if that behavior reflects some perverse, unusual, neurotic or self-destructive trend in his personality?

We suggest an alternative rule of living—a Diamond Rule which comprehends the extraordinary complexity of the interpersonal space and goes beyond the presumptions of "I know what's good, right, ethical and moral for you because it has to be that which I find pleasurable, acceptable and attractive to me."

No. The Golden Rule is entirely too simplistic in these protean times, when we cannot count on uniform wants, desires or responses from our fellows. Observance of such subjective goodness results in such indignations as:

"So Bill hates opera ... couldn't he have been more grateful for season tickets which would enlarge his cultural experiences?"

"How could Mary not have been pleased with the opportunity to speak before the Garden Club? Even if she is shy and timid ... I would have loved the chance!"

"Now how could Matilda not appreciate my giving her last year's evening gown? Uppity maid ... she could find places to wear it if she put her mind to it!"

"Harry's such a prig: wanting Vivaldi instead of Deep Purple. How does he expect to keep up with the times?"

"Such a lukewarm response to my hearty handshake. Even if he did get out of the hospital just last week, following his brain tumor removal, he's got to try to be more social!"

"Imagine Madge turning down my invitation to bridge! Dumb excuse, if you ask me, that her husband just died yesterday … all the more reason for her to get back into circulation!"

Such comments do nothing to improve the interpersonal space. We would do better to ask ourselves:

"Did little Johnnie really want to go to college, or was all the work and struggle I went through aimed at turning Johnnie into someone who fit my model for a successful son?"

"Did I give that party for Jane's pleasure, or because I love to give parties?"

The Diamond Rule dictates that we do *nothing* unto others until we have traversed the space which separates us from the other—walked in his or her moccasins, so to speak—and even then we may only do, reply to, or reject the other's invitation to relate only as we and he find mutually acceptable.

Putting it another way, we are only free to do unto others as our understanding of them allows us to comprehend their needs, quite aside from our own prejudgments, culture and self-interest.

One of the most vulnerable times in our lives is when we are misunderstood in the act of "giving" as we understand giving.

In Helen Merrell Lynd's book *Shame and the Sense of Identity* she describes the young girl hurrying home from school with a papier-mâché necklace, which she enthusiastically drapes around her mother's neck as Mom sits reading the paper. The mother, taken aback as the still-moist glue soils her clean collar, exclaims, "Ugh! Cynthia, what are you doing!" The ensuing moment of shame and guilt experienced by the child—the all too familiar through-the-tears, "I thought you'd like it."—is echoed all too frequently in all our lives.

Gaining true understanding of the wants of others is like compounding away the grit and grime of a reflecting surface so that we may see more of ourselves. It is all too easy to say, "I want an attaché case for Christmas: he wants an attaché case for Christmas," or "I'd love to have one, so I think this food processor would be great in her kitchen," or "Everyone loves cherry stones so let's take them to Carol's clam shack." The fact is that, if we trouble ourselves to assume more awkward and kinky positions in our endeavors to get at the hidden and remote undersurfaces of the lives of the people in our space, the more creatively and artistically are we likely to then be able to see ourselves.

The pollsters seem to know this as they, with E. E. Cummings, quest for the more beautiful answer to the more beautiful questions. The point here is elementary: Do unto others as your genuine effort to understand them produces knowledge of what would be wise, good and correct for them, while at the same time not violating your own beliefs about such similar verities.

The idea that if you understand another you will then be able to give to them or meet their now-discovered needs requires some additional modification because it is not our intent to establish any imperatives in your life. Perhaps the small print at the bottom of the page should read, "If you would like to relate to others in a giving way—then do unto them, etc.," for understanding is not a mandate for giving or yet caring (even though it does often occur that way).

A most frequent comment made by patients has been, "Do you know what I mean?" followed by, "Nobody seems to understand me." To them, this is tantamount to saying, "Nobody cares." Their premise is that if somebody understood he would certainly care and accordingly do something about the patient's plight.

Now, while understanding does not always produce caring or helping, it frequently does lead to caring, often becoming a vital pathway to empathy. And in the process of understanding another, the understander creates a setting in which he himself is both more available for reciprocal understanding and more likely to be liked, loved and self-aware.

It may not be primary that understanding others allows us to like them, but it frequently follows that we do get closer to them, for a dimension of understanding is empathy, and seeing oneself in others.

It does not follow that those who achieve understanding for others are necessarily liked for it. But it is nice to be listened to and surely those understood are inclined to like you. Oftentimes you are experienced as understanding when you do not, if you have merely remained pleasantly and attentively silent, because silence to most means approval. Most people who apparently ask for understanding really want to be affirmed as right, good, correct and justified in their feelings. Their request has this logic: they cannot imagine that anyone who truly understood them could not appreciate that they were justified in their feelings and behavior.

But understanding is not a subcategory of judging. It is perfectly feasible to understand even the most dreadful act without judging it. Understanding is much easier than knowing what (if anything) to do with your understanding. Contrariwise doing something when you don't understand produces less reliable and less successful results than forestalling your action, if possible, until you have achieved some understanding.

What of the situation where you are the woe begotten, deceived, cuckolded, jilted and misunderstood other? Should you turn the other cerebral lobe and forfeit anger, remorse and frustration, while understanding your adversary? To some extent, yes, insofar as a real understanding of the madness, anger, method and meaning of your adversary allows you a better response. There is the possibility that in such an encounter we may discover that we are masochistic in a sado-masochistic relationship and with such a discovery we advance one step closer to our freedom.

For the terrifying truth is that in order for others to do as they do unto us. it is necessary that we be as we are—the takers, the hurters, the martyrs, the long-suffering schlubs—so by all means understand the people who hurt you but for God's sake *don't* turn the other cheek. Instead, turn the other cerebral lobe. For only when you insist on living in their space are you so vulnerable.

Understanding need not keep us in situations which remain painful and draining. To the degree to which we understand someone, we have increased our options of response, and added some which are far more exciting and self-fulfilling than what our primitive gut response is likely to produce, especially on those too-frequent occasions when we are temporarily trapped in a repetition compulsion.

A brief tangent of definition is appropriate here, having used such terms as masochism and repetition compulsion: in a paper called "Beyond the Pleasure Principle," Freud identified the phenomenon wherein people chose the familiar-though-painful over the new-and-probably-pleasurable. This was misconstrued by some to suggest that some people liked pain. This is an inadequate explanation.

What is true is that neurotic psychological inertia often holds us to the familiar, even when it is painful.

This dilemma was most dramatically articulated for me by a young Chinese patient whose parents' restaurant was adjacent to our out-patient clinic at Boston University. Her husband was a heroin addict and she labored endlessly to achieve the meager gains of caring for their infant son and supporting her husband's drug habit. She described herself as being like a trapeze artist who knew that there were many other swings to grab for her salvation, but that in order to grab another she had to let go of the one she was on. And this meant a terrible moment of nothing—that great existential void so poignantly defined by Kierkegaard.

The dialogue which occurs between our emotional and intellectual response is good for us, as is our intellectual awareness of the emotional response.

Yet whereas understanding others may regenerate older relationships with a much higher personal yield, it is not correct to argue that understanding means staying. If beseeching others implore you (erroneously) to understand as a preliminary experience to accepting or loving them, you must then admonish then that that need not necessarily occur. We must be willing to permit our understanding to let go of old relationships before we can generate new and more satisfactory ones!

A serious potential for the converse (not understanding) is anger and rejection. We have all noted such reactions to strange others such as the child, retardate, senile, insane or whomever else confounds our reason. We have been known in such situations to call such an individual barbarian and, as a "stranger," to ostracize him.

Understanding others may often prove to be the most ameliorating enterprise which we can undertake to curtail our own aggressive instincts. The admonishment may read: *either understand others or run the risk of discovering your own brutal capabilities.* However, it is an exciting moment in human interaction to watch a stranger who comes to the village, initially as a threat to our sexual and nutritional security, who then moves through our understanding from "stranger" to "friend." It is an equally interesting sequence to observe in the new relationship of friendship and understanding such things as sacrifice—giving up what is ours for the pleasure of the other person.

So in terms of our own civility, failure to understand others is likely to confront us with our own inherent brutality while success at understanding others may achieve a sublimation of this and ennoble us.

Understanding may be the pathway to empathy and, in the process of understanding another, one often becomes available for reciprocal understanding and loving. But not necessarily. The converse reaction of wrath, anger, rejection and brutality all too often befall those who are not understood and thus considered strange and dangerous.

On a recent William F. Buckley talk show, B. F. Skinner stated that there was no such thing as an inborn moral posture. He reminded the audience of what has been society's moral attitude toward those from whom it has little or nothing to fear—the child, the retardate, the elderly, the mentally deranged and the incurably ill—those who have been the scapegoats of our anger and rage. I should like to add that it is not merely the weakness of such people which seduces us to anger. It is our failure to understand them which intimidates us and turns us to anger and rage.

Thus returning to our prior metaphor of the stranger who begins as a threat, jeopardizing the sexual and nutritional security of the residents—who then moves through understanding to friendship; and after friendship may even elicit the giving up of personal possessions or privileges for the pleasure of another—we are made aware of the extraordinary triumph of culture over appetite, an amazing testimony to the power of learning, when one surrenders one's pleasure not for one's own practical good but for the pleasure of another.

Across the plain of understanding lies the valley of care and loving ... not always, but often enough to encourage us to a more sparkling rule of living.

Perhaps with this new directive we can surrender the baser mental positions of *View #1* and *View #2*, i.e.,

This is what I want to give you so this is what you'll get:
-Mo, I don't care what you do ... I'll continue doing things my way.
-It makes me feel good to give you jewelry and, by damn, you'll *wear* it!
-If you're going to continue coming to the table in your undershirt, I'm not going to cook for you anymore.
-Okay, I'll go to church with you if you'll go bowling with me.
-Look, it was a very creative idea to give me yoga lessons, but what will my mother say if she finds out I'm taking those classes?

And we can focus our giving to allow for:
-I really thought you'd enjoy getting a pet leopard, but I guess I was just projecting my desires. What would you like instead?
-Look, it doesn't matter that your gift to me cost much less than mine to you ... this is what I thought you'd enjoy having, so I enjoyed giving it to you.
-But Darling, I thought you'd be crazy about Indian food ... didn't realize you'd had that unfortunate experience in the Orient. Well, where would you like to eat instead of this place?

8

"I'm Not Your Mother!"

"Memory is a creative process. What an individual seeks
to become determines what he remembers of his has been.
In this sense the future determines the past."

—*Adler*

The Bond

The prototype human experience is called "the bond" and since all understanding is heir to that initial interpersonal union, it is proper to devote a chapter to this phenomenon.

The bond has been called "that enduring tie that unites members of the species into couples."[5] Selma Fraiberg provides a very sensitive insight to how the human mother/child bond becomes the essential instrument for modifying our natural aggressive urges. She points out that natural aggression is never destroyed or abolished in the nurture process; only modified and redirected.

The technique for effecting this redirection is a function of the process of this early bonding. Thus loss of the loved (or hated!) parent by the child can be an emotionally fatal experience, because aggression may be set loose from the early bond if the lost parent or parent-surrogate is not appropriately replaced. Restated: conflicts between the claims of love and aggression are central to an understanding of personality development, and in preserving ones rapport with the nurturing parent, primitive aggression must discover alternative expression. In the loss of such a parent there is less inducement toward this. Efforts to preserve the care and love of this special other is futile, because the fates have taken them.

Although some manage to survive biologically despite such a loss of nurture, a sad breed of humorless robots may emerge and, in instances when the aggression becomes self-directed, a serious and morbid depression may occur.

In a society which has closed its eyes to the phenomenon of child-battering, deprivation and neglect, we have too frequently operated on the false premise

---

5   Konrad Lorenz

53

that all infants and children are provided with a human bond in the course of their formative years. But Fraiberg calls our attention to the so-called diseases of non-attachment, which lead to human behavior disorders more tragic than any of those discovered in the laboratories of Barlow and his motherless apes. Having become unbonded, a primary incapacity to form later human bonds is the dire consequence to the individual. In relating to such an individual one has the eerie feeling of non-contact: a Sahara of interpersonal space. The life histories (psychobiographies) of such individuals reveal that, thus stigmatized, few if any other persons of significance ever enter their experience. With no joy, no grief, no remorse and no guilt, partners can be exchanged as objects with the characteristic of sameness, a designation more seemly for such things as chairs or checkers (*View #1*).

Another terrifying characteristic of such individuals is the total absence of self-observation, self-criticism, and the pathetic failure to be able to receive humor with a smile. What emerges are human vagrants occupying our slums, second-class rooming houses, the back wards of mental institutions, regulars and repeaters in our state prisons, in carnivals and such other world enterprises where the absence of human attachment can afford vocation and specialization. For the women, prostitution affords professional scope for this condition of emotional deadness.

Ms. Fraiberg goes on to point out that this deadness within those individuals often demands powerful psychic jolts for them to affirm their existence. These may frequently take the form of wanton sexual or aggressive acts against anonymous objects who serve the purpose of providing only an echo for the thud of their assault—which somehow redeems these hollow individuals. Once we clarify and appreciate the necessity for a love bond as the instrument to re-direct, tailor and place aggression in the service of the bond rather than destroying it, we recognize that the first important application of the thesis of "How to Understand Somebody Else" is that the first somebody else who must be understood, for a change, is the newborn infant. In order to understand adults it is crucial that we have some awareness of the quality of their early bonding. We must understand, for example, what responses were received to such infant signaling as "I am wet, I am hungry, I am cold, I am untouched." The simple truism here is that when there is no one to read these signs, there is soon no motive to give signals.

The final tragic consequence of lack of response to our signaling can, in fact, lead to "infant suicide," a phenomenon otherwise referred to in the medical literature as marasmus. We learn from the ethologists that many species of animal can wait only so long to be acknowledged for their inner potentials, to be affirmed and expressed by environmental compliment. Even more so are we learning from the clinics and institutions which treat autistic and atypical psychotic children that without initial bonding during the first, second and third years of life people may require years of disciplined professional care to reproduce the salutary effect of a mother's morning smile and the cuddling to her breast.

Our point here is that the bond *is the civilizing* process of newborn infants and that all later human relationships (*repeat—all later human relationships*) take their quality and meaning from these crucial early developmental experiences.

Thus in looking at our adult relationships and in pondering on how to understand somebody else we shall continue to emphasize that a careful understanding of their earliest human relationships is crucial to understanding others. No issue for insight or clarification is more likely to give answers for self or other awareness than are all those interpersonal relationships that formed us for the tasks of social living.

Transference

It would not be an exaggeration to say that every adult human relationship has a significant element of transference from those formative bonding relationships. We are saying very little more here than that the language of human relating is structured into our very being during our first groping contacts with adults. Through our bonding relationships we are forever bound to repeat those styles and methods unless, through the wisdom of hindsight and understanding, we can separate ourselves from these bonding patterns.

We must also comprehend that all of those others who are placed in our spheres of interpersonality probably cannot present us very much more than their former bonding ties allow them. In dealing with them, unless we pause to comprehend the language and alphabet of their childhood experiences, we are unlikely to engage them realistically. The language of human relating is composed of the vowels of successful early human bonds and the consonants of unresolved failures and frustrations in early human relationships.

We may admonish contemporaries to stop treating us as if we were their mother, father, older brother, sister, etc.—but once we grasp that we are not being treated for our contemporary reality and worth but that we are being displaced upon, transferred upon and otherwise distorted by contemporaries (who are in compromising, intimate, threatening, destructive or unworking relationships to us) then can we respond with more realism than otherwise.

We are not asking you to become a psychiatrist ... merely a *student* of the interpersonal territory, a geographer of that space that separates you from your neighbors. Once you discipline your observations to comprehend the issue of transferences with the significant other persons in your life, you will soon be able to discern when the other person speaks from the freedom of "here and now" and when he is bound by his bonding experiences. You will come to know when feeling is original and creative or warmed over and repetitive.

The argument is ultimately simple: At some point in human evolution we lost the skill or genetic endowment for spontaneous self-sufficiency at birth. It came to pass that our survival needs were delivered to us by the giants who conceived and nursed us to maturity. Those agents of nurture were also our mentors of culture. Separation from them was soon discerned as equivalent to our death, for we recognized our involvement with others as a life or death enterprise from the onset of our lives.

How often have we observed adults interacting with their friends and neighbors in petty areas as if their lives depended upon the result! The tragic fact is that for too many, the specter of the survival struggle between ourselves (as infants) and our parents (as providers of life sustaining substances and shelter) is tragically persistently ever present—for the early delivery system was interpersonal!

The infant knew there was food, warmth and air out there—but it had to be delivered, and the deliverers would either be on time or late. If they tarried, the primordial angers and fears surfaced: as they arrive on time, faith, trust and love were formed—and memory will punch in the joys and pains of these innumerable incidents in which tension was followed by relief, hunger by satiety, when cold was met with warmth, wet with dry, and *alone with other*!

Let us proceed with this idea of transference but approach it from an alternate position.

One is asked in the earliest days of psychiatric training to consider this concept and is directed to his personal therapy experiences for capturing its special and particular meaning. In mastering and understanding its complexity, one is baptized as a therapist. Awareness of this phenomenon needs to be provided to the lay person too, for use in his family and social life.

Most human relationships should have their crust of transference stripped away so that people can behave unencumbered by the prejudgments inherent in this process.

Transferring

All of us have personal likes and dislikes, i.e.,

"I have always disliked overweight people."

"So and so makes me feel uncomfortable."

"I can't stand red."

"Ever since I can remember I have always been attracted to people who have such and such a trait."

"Look at the person over there. Doesn't he give you the willies?"

The point is that there are people whose intrinsic and essential worth is obscured by prejudgment. For us to ever properly cross the interpersonal space that separates them from us for "now" relationships, we must be unburdened of such prejudgments.

Transference overlays all those prejudices onto the free flow of interpersonal communication. Encumbered with transferences, we project feelings and judgments from special others in our recent or remote past upon current others. It may be positive or negative.

A Norman Rockwell cover on an old *Saturday Evening Post* showed a husband being yelled at by his employer. In the second caption the husband was shown yelling at his wife who in turn was found in the next caption yelling at her young son. And in the final quadrant the son was observed kicking the dog.

It can be said that the energy of anger, the heat of hostility kindled in the husband but un-discharged through fear, waited in him and found a spillover object—a displacement against his wife who delivered the same anger to the young son who in turn transferred it to the dog. Those moments of sudden and overpowering affection or antipathy toward perfect strangers take their nourishment, find their explanation in the transference phenomenon.

Such a phenomenon may be used to re-define romance and later in this book we shall elaborate on how infatuation and, in many instances so-called love, are in fact merely transference experiences.[6]

---

6   I remember once during my first year of psychiatric training, planning a facetious essay, "How to Make the Most of a Positive Transference." With the skills of a beginning student gleaned from his introductory course in psychiatry, I had designs to apply what I was learning in a practical and direct way toward a more successful social and dating life. What an interesting full circle it is for me, at this point in my career, to be approaching that same subject in this form. I am still convinced that a proper understanding of our transference relationships with others is a crucial component for achieving quality relationships to them, though at this point I feel less enterprising about the use of this understanding.

To test the strength and content of your own early bonding, ask yourself:
"Are others capable of giving me pleasure or pain?"
"Do I tend to anticipate pleasure or pain from others?"
"Is my 'set' such that I expect:

Total obedience? *(View #1)*
Complete, predictable cooperation in a given area? *(View #2)*
An unpredictable and wide range of responses, all geared toward
some other goal than to give me pleasure or pain?" *(View #3)*

Now test your transferences:
"When someone does or says something that creates pain for me, is my first response one of aggression—or do I seek an explanation or understanding of the motive, believing that my pain was probably only an accidental result and not the main reason for the act?"

"When it becomes clear to me that another's response to me has less to do with my actions than the actions of some early loved one (or hated one!) in his or her life, am I able to understand this inability to respond to me, and what do I do about it?"

"When an interaction results in emotions in me that are much stronger than the interaction justifies, am I able to trace back to my 'set' which touched off this reaction?"

"Do I know *why* I hate the color green; become furious when someone forgets my first name; feel sorrow and pain (which I may translate into anger) when someone removes his or her shoes in my presence?"

"When I enter into contact with another, bringing along emotions from prior interactions, do I vent these prior emotions on that other and then try to justify them?" exclaiming:

With *View #1:*
-I'm used to being treated this way, so that's how you are to treat me.
-I don't care how your father addressed your mother!
-Who cares if it would make you happy?

With *View #2:*
-But how can you expect that of me when you never do it?
-Okay, if you'll do it, so will I.

-But that wouldn't be proper ... what will people say?

Or With *View #3:*

-I understand that you're not used to doing things like that, but I'd appreciate your trying for my sake.

-I don't give a damn if it's reciprocal or not. Try to understand that our needs are not the same.

-Well, obviously it's not working the spontaneous way, so shall we formulate an agreement on what you'll do and what I'll do, and forget about our old patterns?

9

How Could They Do That to Me?

It is not that the patient transfers from former to present, but that because of his limitations in perceptions and relatedness he perceives relationships with distortion.

Let us now inquire into the meaning of another comment so frequently heard during a failing interpersonal relationship. "I can't understand how they could do that to me!"

Begin with "to me!" and try to understand that most people do things to and for themselves, not "*to*" others. It is an often erroneous presumption to assume the behavior of another as a "to me" behavior.

One may more precisely say, "When you do that I feel badly," but the challenge that because I feel badly you should not do that is more often than not an erroneous presumption. This chapter will explore this issue of narcissism in interpersonal relationships and will seek to reveal how often we believe we operate in the best interests of others only to find, in rejection, it was our *own* satisfaction we sought.

Indulge me briefly in the well worn but endless resource of calling upon the Jewish mother for guidance and insight here:

Son: Hello, Mom. I'm so happy. Everything you ever told me was good and pleasing, and life-affirming has occurred. I'm in medical school studying to be a specialist and I have found a girl who makes me very happy. She seems to respect my needs for privacy when I study, is very undemanding, an excellent cook, is magnificent in bed, gorgeous and sensitive and in her own right quite intelligent and self-sufficient.

Mother: (long pause) Is she Jewish?

Son: No.

Mother: (longer, perhaps eternal, pause) How could you do that to me?

The son has cooked his own goose by telling his mother that her wisdom and advice has always led to his success and happiness. He agrees that Mama is always right. And based on this, he has made Mama the ultimate judge of the correctness of his choices.

In asking, "How could you do this to me," Mama is saying that her son's choice of a woman seriously undermines the entire value system she has spent years and years teaching him: that in making this choice he is betraying her love, sacrifices and motherly efforts to guide him toward his own greatest good. He is defying the relationship duties implicit in her View #2 expectations from him!

She can now affirm that the failure of his father's business; the crash of the stock market; the sinking of San Francisco into the San Andreas Fault and Golda Meier's hypertension will all follow as a direct result of this son's betraying movement away from all that is good and right. And the son, agreeing that she knows what is good and right, is now engulfed by a tidal wave of guilt and self-incrimination.

By implanting this guilt response in her son at an early age, the mother can now harvest this extremely sensitive reaction from him to her approval or disapproval. The forever-dependent child in him responds to the guilt-inducing disapproval of Mama to his adult decision. He is now engaged in a dramatic internal battle between his acceptance of his mother's value system (View #2) and his belief in his own adult decision-making capacities (View #3).

Guilt Responses

The mechanism of guilt appears to be quite simple: the combination of the child's *lust* for forbidden fruit plus the *fear* of retaliation by powerful protectors or aggressors. How quickly these guilt-ghosts of childhood can be reincarnated in adulthood indicates the degree to which the adult still responds to the guilt mechanisms trained into him or her during childhood.

The determining factor in one's guilt response quotient is the degree to which the illogical, unthinking guilt reaction (to parental labeling of a "no-no") becomes replaced by an ability to decide for oneself whether or not there has been a real violation of a rational adult ethic chosen by the now-adult non-child. (This thing I want is good and right and does not contradict my value system. Therefore, labeling it a "no-no" is ridiculous.)

Third-Party Ghosts

In order to understand others and to relate to them in a healthy, constructive way, we often have to search out some "third party" ghosts who lurk in the minds of those others, whispering to them judgments about *our* behavior as well as their own—setting guidelines of behavior and labeling certain actions as "correct and nice" and other actions as "selfish and cruel."

It is helpful in understanding others to know who these third-party ghosts are and how importantly they influence our relationships with the people who carry these ghosts around inside of them.

This may be no more complex a detecting job than realizing, in the case of the Jewish mother and her son, that the guilt handed to the son may have been a guilt that Mama received from her own father about the evil and harm resulting to a Jew from marrying a Gentile.

The point to identify here is how the vaccination of guilt at an early age can be harvested for a reaction from the always-dependent child in us at the wanton discretion of the adult bearer of guilt allergens unless we understand the process. How quickly these ghosts of history come to life is surely an indicator to quantify one's coefficient of guilt (*View #2* response). In understanding others whom we would like to believe we relate to in a View #3 relationship, there often lurks ghosts of third-party others who label our behavior "correct and nice" or "selfish and cruel"; in understanding others it is surely helpful to know who these folks are and how important is their influence.

For whereas a situation may appear to be dyadic (*View #3*), in order to have a guilt potential a triangle is necessary and the "secret" third *can be* discovered. When he or she is found and their key role noted, both parties may be tremendously relieved. To the untutored observer it is usually quite difficult to detect the presence of the secret third—when your wife has had an argument with her mother, has been intimidated by her father, has been spoken to harshly by your secretary, or has been gossiping with her girlfriend, etc., the ghost of that experience spreads its veil over your supper conversation—yet without some guidance to this phenomenon you are significantly compromised in your effort to understand anybody.

Most important relationships are triangular, consisting of you, the other, plus special third-person ghosts whose relationships to this other is unresolved either by a recent awakening stress or by enduring persistence without current provocation.

10

The Mechanisms of Defense

*"Anxiety is the dizziness of freedom. It is the emotion
of some potentiality crying to be born."*

—*Kierkegaard*

Most people don't do, feel, think or say what they would like to. Some do. Neither category of people can be said to be healthy (mentally) for this alone.

Those who don't may consciously know this, and what they don't do, think, feel or say is consciously suppressed and can be called out at will.

Some people do not know, feel, think, say or act as they would wish to and don't know it because the thoughts, feelings, actions or words are unconsciously repressed. The process of repression may not be completely adequate. When it is not, such people know that something is troubling them because they feel anxious without knowing why.[7]

Some people appear as if they were feeling, thinking, saying or acting as they wish or prefer to, but in fact they are not. Trying to understand those people—behaving, thinking and feeling as if they were really that way—brings us to the essential message that what they are really doing is defending against their underlying selves by an extraordinary variety of mechanisms, which can be discerned.

In so defending they are trying to avoid the anxiety of conflict between what is and what they wish to be. In order to proceed further with our discussion of the mechanisms of defense we need some historical prologue on this issue of anxiety and conversion hysteria, for it is from these concepts that flows the whole

---

7   There is one unusual circumstance when someone behaves in a way that they ostensibly would not want to. We would expect them to be very upset by this but in fact they are not. They demonstrate a so-called *la belle indifference*, an inappropriate casualness about their behavior. This occurs in the conversion hysterias reported upon by Freud and Brewer in 1898 when individuals presented to their physicians central nervous system symptoms such as paralysis or blindness. The reasoning behind such conversions is that if they don't "see" or "act out" their unacceptable wishes, they are safe. Why people behave this way may be oversimplified to the generalization that it will result in more pain than pleasure. This, of course, includes the pains of retaliation by real or imagined others who will not like what they say, feel, think or do, and will hurt or punish them for this.

65

Freudian literature and most of our current psychodynamic formulations of the human condition.

Anxiety is almost universally accepted as the signaling symptom of internal psychic conflict. It was initially construed as the fallout of energy when primitive *id* sexual wishes met either the real prohibitions of society at large or society internalized as *super-ego*. Soon it became apparent that keeping the lid on other unconscious wishes, feelings or drives—the so-called id forces such as hostility—could also produce anxiety, and the psychic mechanisms studied as techniques for dealing with this were repression and conversion.

Repression is the automatic and seemingly effortless and involuntary relegation of consciously repugnant or intolerable ideas, feelings, wishes, motives, beliefs and impulses into non-awareness (the so-called "unconscious"). Anxiety is noted as the active force which accomplishes this.

When the process is not complete there is leakage outside and one experiences anxiety.

All too frequently the process is incomplete and there is leakage or spillage of the anxiety without awareness of the source, ideas or feelings. When the process is complete there may occur a somatic alliance and some body function is altered. When this occurs the condition is termed "conversion."[8]

Anxiety is not only manageable by repression or conversion. There are many other mechanisms which serve this crucial purpose.[9] Let's begin our discussion of the most pertinent among them by paraphrasing Laughlin's definition:

Though first given credibility and professional status by French and Austrian physicians, the processes were not unknown to the ancient Greeks who comprehended them under the term "hysteria." Their view (poignantly simple) was that the uterus (pronounced huterus) had become loosened from its moorings in the pelvis and was wandering in the body (if not actually, symbolically).

Their view that the disease was primarily one of women was inherent in this formulation and, though wrong in this respect, they were right to appreciate that unfulfilled or unsatisfied sexuality symbolized by a wandering huterus was the root cause of the symptoms of anxiety and physical weakness or paralysis.

---

8   Conversions most often affect the neurosensory system or involuntary musculature and thus patients present such complaints as blindness, paralysis and/or weakness.

9   These have been most extensively surveyed by Henry P. Laughlin in his classic text, *The Neuroses*.

This notion of "repressed" ideas or feelings causing symptoms did not lie dormant between the age of Greek medicine and the Freudian literature. It was in fact carefully noted in the writings of Pierre Janet in the several decades before Freud journeyed to Paris to study with his student, the famous Charcot. His concept was that of a "fixed idea" locked in the subconscious recesses of the mind. His theories of how or why this was so are not germane at this time. What was more relevant to Janet and Charcot was how to get them out, and for this they medicalized the animal magnetism techniques of their fellow Frenchman Anton Mesmer and so was born the technique of medical hypnotism for the relief of mental illness.

It is alleged (perhaps anecdotally) that Freud, while witnessing a demonstration of the new technique wherein a confused subject was trying to understand why he had opened his umbrella in a lecture hall, perceived that the post-hypnotic suggestion could indeed be extricated from the subject's mind if instead of probing directly for it he could be persuaded to free associate in his quest for the answer; and it worked. He then concluded that if post-hypnotic suggestions can be discovered by free association then why not "fixed ideas" or "repressed" feelings, particularly those underlying conversion hysteria; and so was born the psychoanalytic method.

A mental mechanism is a specific intrapsychic or intrapersonal process operating outside of and beyond conscious awareness, through use of which a resolution of emotional conflict and freedom from anxiety is sought and realized independently or as a reinforcement for repression. While conscious attempts to secure relief from emotional tensions and avoidance of the pain of uncomfortable feelings may be similarly named, it is not a mechanism of defense unless it occurs unconsciously and out of awareness.

Not only must we be alert to the human propensity to protect ourselves from unbearable inner feelings and ideas, but from external stress and pain as well.

And as the external world, during our growth and development, becomes progressively more important as a source of pleasure and interest, the more opportunity there is for pain and thus the greater necessity to learn how to allow only acceptable amounts of the external world in.

A preliminary effort may be merely to distort our perceptions to meet with our personal needs rather than to comply with the starkness of our external environment. But when our defenses are focused on constricting the external input by such techniques as denial, delusion or hallucination, we are involved in regressions which are subsumed under the overall term, psychosis. The value of this text will be quite limited for understanding those so encumbered—for our focus is on facilitating relationships between those who, for all practical purposes, live in the "same world."

Following is a list of mental mechanisms. You can hardly be expected on the basis of this text to professionally identify these defenses in your neighbors and yourself. We only acquaint you with these facts to point out that such processes exist so that you may include their possibilities in your efforts to understand friends and neighbors. We'll be harking back to this material throughout our text and, through anecdote, you will finally grasp the significance of these processes in your daily life.

A List of Mental Mechanisms

1. *Compensation*

A mental mechanism in which the individual attempts to make up for, to over-compensate for, real or fantasized deficiencies in his physique, performance, skills or psychological attributes; i.e., someone with one lung or a hare lip becoming a renowned trumpet player; someone with childhood palsy becoming a marathoner.

2. *Displacement*

A mental mechanism in which an emotional feeling is transferred from its internal locus to an external object; i.e., phobia of the marketplace (agoraphobia) whereby one displaces onto extreme crowds an internal fear of having to deal with his sexuality or hostility; or, as Little Hans of Freud's famous casebook chose, instead of coping with the overwhelming awareness of his sexual interest in his mother and the forbidding relationship to his father, to displace his fear to horses—thereby could he dismiss the entire matter from his awareness. In such instances secondary processes such as generalizations may also occur, in which the phobia transfers to all animals or extends even beyond to such things as the outdoors of the places where animals may reside.

3. *Dissociation*

A mental mechanism whereby the emotional significance or affect is split off, detached from an idea or event. Its most exaggerated manifestation may occur in fainting, where one not merely psychologically dissociates but actually physiologically leaves.

4. *Idealization*

A mental mechanism in which an object or person is emotionally overvalued or aggrandized not in accord with his or her real attributes or liabilities but with the needs of the observer; i.e., "Butter would melt in her mouth."

5. *Incorporation*

A mental mechanism wherein another person (or parts thereof) are incorporated and experienced and related to as one's own, such as in *depression* when one has intolerable or unmanageable feelings toward an external object and, through *introjection*, directs them within—toward the self, albeit severely suffering themselves in the process.

6. *Identification*

A mental mechanism by which one makes oneself like another. This process may be positive if the other is admired, but is as often negating when the identification is with someone who is actually disliked or feared. In the latter category we call it "identification with the aggressor." We often see children disliking certain traits of their parents and relatives, but pathologically and unconsciously drawn to mime them in their adult lives … because nurture abhors a vacuum and we can't grow up to be a not-someone.

Further examples of identification with the aggressor are the child acting as ghost, scaring his neighbors as a mechanism of warding off his own fears.

7. *Introjection*

A mental mechanism whereby we take into ourselves what we perceive to be the other's feelings about us: hating those who we think hate us or trying to make those fear us who we fear, as would a child playing doctor or dentist trying to ward off his apprehension about his next visit to the dentist.

An interesting secondary elaboration of introjection is introjection of the authorities who we are intimidated by, and then projecting that intimidation onto others via an exaggerated intolerance of them or an exaggerated punitive approach. Some have suggested that this was the mechanism exercised by the vehement protagonists of prohibition.

8. *Inversion*

A mental mechanism whereby a specific unacceptable or disavowed wish; impulse; affect or drive; attitude; complex or motive is directly reversed, i.e., love for hate, respect for disdain; i.e., an unconsciously hated other may appear loved and indulged. A child who has been jealous and hostile toward his mother may often capitulate to an equally zealous overindulgence and allegiance to Mom. A spinster daughter may appear to be the most giving of daughters, only to be revealed in psychoanalysis as harboring unbearable death wishes against her mother.

9. *Rationalization*

A mental mechanism wherein one justifies or attempts to make tolerable impulses or needs or feelings or behaviors or motives which are unacceptable: substituting a false but reasonable motive for one's real and reprehensible ones.

10. *Symbolization*

A mental mechanism whereby one attributes an undue degree of emotional meaning to a neutral external object; i.e., a security blanket.

11. *Sublimination*

A mental mechanism by which instinctual drives which are consciously unacceptable, blocked or unobtainable are re-channeled, and redirected to secure their disguised external expression in a socially and personally acceptable fashion through creative endeavor.

12. *Turning Against the Self*

A mental mechanism also termed masochism, more often seen in our culture among women but hardly rare in men. The scenario goes something like this: The daughter or son establish an all-too-early misunderstanding and attitude against the parents for an often arbitrary set of faults. Early on the affect may be released in naughtiness or general unruliness, but always with the awareness that too vehement a release of this energy is not without the real or imagined hazard of abandonment and death. Therefore something must be done with this anger; so it is turned against the self, allowing self-accusations and feelings of unworthiness to prevail despite manifest arguments to the contrary. The possessors of this mechanism then proceed into situations which allow a persistence of those feelings, i.e., bad marriages, bad jobs, etc.

13. *Projection*

Projection is one of the more complex and interesting mental mechanisms and will be given a somewhat more elaborate treatment than those previously mentioned because in the process of understanding projection one may come to a richer understanding of those other mental mechanisms already cited.

Projection and its several subtypes is an interesting mix of several mechanisms already noted and deserves special attention. Its dictionary definition is: a mental mechanism operating outside of and beyond conscious awareness whereby the consciously disowned aspects of the self are rejected or disowned and thrown outward, to become imputed to others. The attributes which are so assigned to another are real to the projector, who reacts and responds to them accordingly.

Sigmund Freud in the famous Schreber case[10] noted a striking example of projection in paranoia when he observed, "an internal perception is suppressed and its content, after undergoing a certain kind of distortion, instead enters consciousness in the form of an external perception. Thus I see not what is without but what is within, projected upon what is without."

Freud pointed out that the initial proposition for this paranoid male was "I, a man, love him (a man)." Because such a view in full consciousness would be intolerable it was first altered to its reverse, i.e., "I, a man, hate him (a man)."

Though the internal perception of this feeling was less noxious or toxic, it was still not a bearable idea or affect and so Schreber went to a tertiary elaboration of reversal in which he stated, "'He hates me' which, of course, justifies my hating him and believing that he is after me and persecuting me and further confounds the possibility that 'I love him' the original idea and affect which the ego finds unbearable." He went on to show how three additional aspects of the "I love you" statement can be altered by mechanisms of defense: (1) In delusions of *jealousy* one may alter the subject—not "I love him" but "She (the she being my wife or girlfriend) loves or lusts for him," and thus I become jealous and suspicious of her; (2) In *erotomania* which alters the object—not "I love him" but "I love her ... and her and her," etc.; and (3) The final configuration, *megalomania*, which rejects the entire proposition, i.e., "I do not love at all. I do not love anyone except myself."

---

10   In 1903, Daniel Paul Schreber, an appeals court judge in Dresden, Germany, a man of superior mental gifts and endowed with an unusual keenness of intellect and observation, published his autobiography, *Memoirs of My Nervous Illness*. Countering the efforts of friends to restrain him from such an endeavor he preferred in his words to "close my eyes to the difficulties which would appear to lie in the path of publication ... so that qualified authorities could hold some inquiry into my personal experiences." So it was that in 1911 Sigmund Freud published his *Psycho-Analytic Notes on an Autobiographical Account of a Case of Paranoia*, the now famous Schreber case. Chapter 3 of this paper is subtitled "The Mechanism of Paranoia" wherein we meet for the first definitive time in the Freudian literature the conceptual formulation of the mechanism of defense called "projection."

What the projective mechanism reveals is that often what we judge to be the behavior or feelings of others is our projections upon them.

Can you believe it? Can you believe that people actually do those things? Well, come with us now through the rest of our text and you will see that we are talking not about them but about us. Yes, outsight will produce insight and in understanding somebody else for a change you will see that the change is in you; not "There but for the grace of God go I," but "There by the grace of wisdom go I," or as Carson McCullers so poetically taught, "There is the I of me."

> *"Anxiety is not an affect among others, it is the threat of imminent non-being. It is not something we have, it is something we are."*
>
> —*Kurt Goldstein*

An Essay on Humor

Though humor cannot be properly defined as a mechanism of defense, it is a quite pertinent device for dealing with those same extremely troublesome inner feelings. So it is fitting that we also discuss humor, laughter and jokes.

Beyond the elemental basic training of all good physicians, a psychiatrist must possess two special traits: (1) he must love a good story, and (2) he must have a sense of humor. Without these two characteristics he will be either bored into oblivion or seduced into his own counter-transference madness.

Martin Grotjahn, in his book on laughter, humor and clowns, shared his poignant awareness of the reversed oedipal situation of most clowns. It remains for me one of the most persuasive arguments for the validity of applying the psychoanalytic method to more than the therapy of mental illness.

We all know that the classic resolution of the so-called Oedipus complex is that the young son, appreciating the foolhardiness of a direct confrontation with his more powerful father and the possibility of serious injury (perhaps genital) in such an endeavor, relinquishes his wish to take away the mother/wife for himself with the resolve that someday he will grow up and be as strong as his father and then get a wife of his own.

He is then free for the more relaxed enterprise of proceeding with acculturation, the assuming of new values and learning the prevailing rights and wrongs without further conflict on this crucial issue.

What of the situation where the father appears not as powerful and sexual with clear prerogatives of supremacy over the son for the favors of the mother but is weak, inept, stupid and bumbling? We are describing clowns: men with large trousers, baggy and loose as if devoid of genitals … men with ties revealing short cut-off ends (need I say more) … grown men uncoordinated, unable to walk without falling, making childish noises and honking funny horns—Dagwood Bumsteads, Archie Bunkers, Red Skeltons, Milton Berles, bedraggled and overwhelmed by the women in their lives. Laughable, not fearful, they are unlikely to prevail in any contest. Dr. Grotjahn puts laughter and aggression in a juxtaposition which no longer allows us to observe or experience anything funny without wondering, "And what hidden aggression (not only oedipal but all aggressions) is here resolved or sublimated?"

In Grotjahn's own words: "Laughter is based on a free release of aggression in a form which is socially acceptable."

All jokes must carry aggression so well disguised and so elegantly expressed as to not interfere with our conscious censorship of open hostility. However, the joke has to be told to someone who confirms the humor by laughter. Otherwise, it may be experienced without disguise as the underlying hostility.

"That's not funny!" or "What's so funny about that!" are remarks usually heard when anger has been poorly masked and the receiver has experienced the anger below when someone has "tried" to be funny. Our quest in understanding others shall be "What do they find funny?" Can they see humor in the world and absurdity around them, or must they hold so fast to their anger as to not allow it an escape even through the vehicle of laughter?

Freud knew this to be the case. He took a special interest in so-called Jewish joking, where he saw quite another attribute of humor. Not only is it an escape for aggression against others but an escape from aggression against the self. It is a masochistic discharge and indulgence. In a way it says, "You do not need to attack me—I can attack myself better than you!"

Grotjahn goes on in his writings to explain, "Because of the double-edged character of wit, its disguise must be delicate—first to keep the thrill of aggression and second to avoid the shame, guilt or embarrassment of an over-communication.

In Freud's 1905 paper on "The Purpose of Jokes," he said: "A joke will allow us to exploit something ridiculous in our enemy which we could not bring forth openly. It will bribe the hero with its yield of pleasure into taking sides with us." In a 1927 paper on humor he added this new dimension by saying: "Humor is not resigned—it is rebellious. It signifies the triumph of the self and the pleasure principle against the unkindness of real circumstances." Here he was pointing out that the humorist is exquisitely sensitive to the world's misery and his own absurd plight, but he triumphs over it in pretense with comic irreverence.

This notion of triumph over real misery with comic pretense is frequently applicable to the looking at self which is what psychotherapy is made of.

At a cocktail party a guest spied James Joyce. He rushed over and exclaimed, "Oh, Mr. Joyce, I feel so privileged to meet you." "Oh," replied Joyce, "have you read my work?" "Oh, to be sure. I'm reading *Ulysses* for the third time now." "Really," Joyce retorted, "and tell me, what do you think of it." "Well," the guest replied, "I don't feel quite ready to comment until I have given it more study." Joyce said in disappointment, "Didn't you think it was funny?"

A patient came to a recent therapy session obviously depressed and more apprehensive about *us* than on her prior several visits. It wasn't long before she accused me of having "laughed at her" during her prior visit. In that session she had recounted an embarrassing incident of her childhood when a school toilet had refused to flush and she had been filled with shame over her dilemma of how to proceed. When she got back to her classroom she convulsed into tears and had to be taken from the room, believing that her secret was known to all and that they were laughing at her.

That very same day an unusually attractive coed talked about hating herself and not wanting anyone to see or touch her body. She went on to recount being a *fat*—"I mean fat"—child and the cruelty of both children and adults about her portliness. She was now in therapy because of her resultant sexual frigidity.

What gave tragedy to both these women's adult lives was that neither had learned to see their childhood experiences as being a bit funny. There was no escape. That was the terrible way it was and is and shall remain.

I wanted desperately to shake the humor into each story. I can envisage that timid, desperately frightened child in the girls' room of PS21 thinking all the gods on Olympus were her convulsively laughing audience. I wondered if she, now a grown woman, would ever allow a smile to incise the boil of those congealed memories.

You can imagine the chagrin of my patient if she thought that I, too, were such an observer. Yet somewhere between the ridicule of laughing at someone and the friendly appreciation of the humor and absurdity of life, lies a path for the working therapist—and for you as an observer and understanding other.

Ionesco, Beckett, Albee, Genet, Pinter, and Weiss are playwrights and poets of this absurdity. Their works follow that extremely popular show, still popular as recently as 1815 in the hospital at Bethlehem, when lunatics could be seen for a penny on Sundays. Maribeau tells us that in pre-revolutionary France the insane were displayed like curious animals to the first simpleton willing to pay a coin.

In Esquirol's 1838 text, *Des Malades Mentales*, he tells of Coulmise, director of Charenton Asylum, organizing performances of the inmates—was this sadism or psychodrama? Who now can answer for him? But the fact is that somewhere in the tragedy of lost souls must be found the humor of resurrection.

"Do not glory in your state if you are wise and civilized men—an instant suffices to disturb and annihilate that supposed wisdom of which you are so proud; an unexpected event, a sharp and sudden emotion of the soul will abruptly change the most reasonable and intelligent man into a raving idiot.[11]

Which brings us to the final point. Not only is our misery absurd but our largess as well, and if we ever forget the humor and absurdity of our state of good health, wealth, family and land, we will be destroyed in its inevitable loss. As a psychiatrist I feel particularly conversant with this truth.

And in this ludicrously large universe surely full of more space than substance, more terror than caring, whether we depart from dust to dust, soul to soul, man to woman, or des oxyribonucleic acid to des oxyribonucleic acid, "If it is nothing else," as Joyce said to his intimidated young admirer, "it's got to be funny—as is me trying to tell you something and you buying my book to find out what it is."

---

11   Mathey, a Geneva physician.

11

Freedom and Changing

"Decision produces knowledge. Not as the patient gets more and more knowledge and insight will he make appropriate decisions but rather as he makes decisions so is he then able to present himself insight and knowledge."

—*Allan Wheelis*

In the conduct of my medical-psychiatric practice over the years, I have frequently been called upon to explain what the results of psychotherapy are likely to be and how it works.

In answering I have explored all the metaphors and nuances of meaning which I could drain from the medical model. In more recent years I have come to see mental illness not as a *medical* experience generally, but as *bondage*, with therapy constructed on the formula of relief.[12]

Let me expand upon this by first explaining the distinction between therapy and counseling or guidance.

Therapy begins when good advice fails. Suggestion, more information and persuasion are delightful and surely efficient mechanisms for getting a person away from one way of looking at a problem or dealing with a situation into another. But when they reply, "I know, I know, but don't you understand I just can't do it?" usually what they mean is not "I can't" but "I'm not free to behave or feel or think otherwise."

We will here discuss this experience of a lack of freedom to be otherwise, and the problems of changing to become otherwise.

There is an exciting contradiction which we will identify at the outset by sharing with you a vignette of a marriage counseling situation, in which a couple were assessing their essential merits and assets in an attempt to reconcile or "try again."

---

12   I appreciate that in those stark organic conditions where there is serious alteration of the functioning of the central nervous system one must, of course, adhere to medical formulations. But this text is designed to concern itself more with the sub-category of mental illness called neurosis and character disorders and, in situations where such conditions have been properly diagnosed, much of the medical material is inadequate to the task of comprehending such derangement.

He included in his virtues sexual fidelity, to which she replied, "That's no big deal because you have no choice." With her terse and cryptic retort she identified a really serious issue; for she was saying, "It's no problem, no chore, no big deal, no great effort for you to be sexually faithful because that's the way you are and it would be harder for you to be unfaithful than remain faithful. So therefore in giving fidelity you do not give, sacrifice or strain yourself in any way; you do it easily and naturally. Whereas if you asked me to curb my drinking or spending habits you'd be asking me to give up something which I really enjoy. So to be even in our bartering, the issue is *how much pain* do we each endure in making a change, not how comparatively serious are our separate liabilities as perceived by the other."

We have thus identified in this exchange the intriguing phenomenon of the *pain of change* rather than severity of misbehavior:

"I will stop chewing gum if you will keep the air conditioner at 70°."

"I will leave a clean bathroom if you will have dinner ready at 6:30."

"I will take Sally to school if you will take my shirts to the cleaners."

These all sound like simple exchanges and none of them seem loaded. But try these now:

"I will entertain your mother if you will stop having lunch with Fred."

"I will relax my discipline with our teenage daughter if you will increase yours with our younger son."

The things up for barter may look equivalent to the neutral observer but they in fact may be profoundly different.

What we are wending our way toward is the philosophical distinction between necessary and *essential* properties vs. ancillary or *secondary* properties. What we are driving at is to separate those characteristics to which people attach identity from those superficial traits which they consider embellishments to their essential identity.

There are some things which we associate with our selfness. *Now while it may be a virtue to not be free to give up one's nuclear integrity, it is a virtue to be able to flex and bend in one's orbit.* What the difference is, in ourselves and others, is the issue upon which the remainder of this chapter shall turn.

Once an individual has established his personal and private understanding of those self-traits which he considers his essentialness, he secludes himself in an identity from which becoming *other* than himself seems not to be the virtue of freedom but the liability of forfeiting integrity. On the other hand to have all of one's behavior—from the widest margins of one's minutest experiences and performance—integrated and held as essential identity components makes a person so rigid and gross in his presentation that he can only be related to as a solid object, incapable of the give-and-take potential which enriches all human interpersonal activity.

In understanding others, what asset and what virtue could be more useful to us in foretelling our future friendship and loveship with them than to have a true sense of what they can sacrifice in the interpersonal give-and-take, and what they must cling to and clutch to as unchangeable and immovable in the inventory of their essential properties?

What we are discussing is one's freedom to perform in the interpersonal space.

In each moment of interpersonal contact, one might inquire of the other, "Is he or she free to be otherwise in this regard?" I submit that this is the most vital question in the realm of the interpersonal.

One couple I counseled had significant disagreements about the virtue of predictability. She fancied herself as a "here and now" person, doing as she pleased when she pleased: some days flighty, others profound; some days socially awake and caring, others flagrant and arrogant. Her partner on the other hand was a man of promise and commitment, full of ideals and a binding sense of duty. If he said he would do a certain thing, then he would. Guilt and depression were his cape. Were either of them free? Only in the long run, only in vertical analysis, did their essential truths emerge.

Her life, a dance of constant unpredictability, was performed on a thin-floored, narrow stage. Her fate was to always be responsive in only a few ways. He on the other hand was able to play randomly on the weekends of his life because he had kept his agreements while at work.

There are also those people who enjoy much freedom though they perpetually patrol the borders of their lives. They stay on the edge—backs strained, nostrils flared, taunt to the tether, choked daily—far from their central moorings. Whereas their work may go forward within their margins and whereas they may play and frolic close to the center post of their lives, they seem to prefer or are taunted by others to journey to their limits.

I am reminded of that German proverb, "If you don't want to know you have a leash around your neck, don't pull on it."

Given all these individual variables, what then is the best preliminary measure we can take of the individual whom we would choose to understand?

The issue raised and considered is simply this: can and do people change and if so, how so?

What sits behind this inquiry of our essential goal of understanding others is that the likelihood of their changing and the hope of their changing is so often crucial to understanding our relationship to them.

The existential psychologists and philosophers have the concept of *becoming* as an alternative to the concept of *being*. Others by their view are in a process of becoming in an also changing world rather than being merely present and here.

To the extent that you discern another in either of these two categories you have drawn a very special conclusion. More so, if you judge one to be in the former condition of becoming, you are thus committed to some notion of the direction in which he/she might be headed. Likewise are you (though somewhat less consciously) committed to holding others responsible for their immediate and past behavior.

I recall reading in a *TIME* magazine article on "the middle years" of a dentist in Connecticut who was interrogated on the question of why he chose to go to dental school. He replied that *he* had not decided to go to dental school; but that some adolescent young junior at Brown University at a time in that boy's life when that option seemed like the most realistic with his minimal resources made that important decision. And that he (the dentist) is now living with that decision as with hundreds of others made by that same fellow. Our dentist in question reflected with sensitivity about the plight of that young chap and seemed reconciled to his inheritance. He spoke with resolution of his sense of continuity and persistence in time with that young fellow and as a contemporary practicing dentist felt they were the same person.

Though it was Dr. Chisholm[13] who made a science of the enterprise for me, it is an extremely practical medical-psychiatric issue to ponder whether our patients are the same persons who behaved in the way they behaved at fixed points in their recent and remote past.

One area that comes to mind promptly is the alcoholic who protests the next morning that it was the alcohol which was speaking, not he. Far more tragic are the inmates of jails for whom either toxic amnesia or psychosis blunt their recollection

---

13   In a course at Brown University some years ago with the distinguished metaphysician Roderick Chisholm, I had occasion to, for the first time since undergraduate years, consider with him and selected graduate students such issues as the continuity of the self in time and concepts of essential human and object properties.

on the day after heinous crimes. I must facilitate their dreadful and painful path backwards to the moment of continuity between their psychotic selves, their criminality, and their current varied states of remorse, shame or indifference.

But why go to such stark extremes when the point is available in the vignettes and anecdotes of everyday simple living? Emerson and other philosophers have goaded us to misconstrue the meaning and worth of personal consistency, calling it the hobgoblin of average minds and contrasting it with the creativity and the excitement of artists and genius. From our point of view, however, the measure of personal consistency in the lives of special others is an absolutely crucial dimension for assessing their worth and compatibility to us in the long run of our human relationship to them.

Whereas philosophers may ponder and play with the notions that all things flow and nothing is, it behooves us surely in our interpersonal lives to quest for a notion of the predictable phenomena traits, qualities, actions and reactions of those with whom we propose to have endearing and enduring human relationships.

Not knowing what romantic turn, what lustful excitement or creative enterprise our mistress or our lover may assign us or create for us—what poem, what metaphor, what exquisite journey into romantic separation from reality he may conceive—is the joy and the poetry of the human experience *in the short run*. But aside from those momentary excursions the sure knowledge that wherever and how long he takes us, we may play there—that truth, virtue, reliability, tenderness and loving will somehow persist and be present in the business of the next day—is a far more viable human commodity than what may romantically fill the interludes.

The quality of a successful human relationship derives from the continuity of those traits and virtues which both partners have judged to be the essential loved and respected properties of the other person. It is an all but impossibly thankless and exhausting project to successfully consummate a human relationship with someone who says "When I feel such and such a way I adhere to such and such an ethic but when I feel another way, I adhere to an alternate ethic," or who admonishes us that promises made on Monday may be invalidated by the vicissitudes of Wednesday which may then account for betrayals on Friday. To identify one's partner or loved one as a role player for whom each role has its separate ethic, each role its separate alliances and each role its separate gamesmanship or rule plan, provides an obstacle course for that human relationship which is beyond resolution.

The difference in our partners between having many costumes, playing many roles, having a wide repertoire of behavior as opposed to being many people is a distinction that it behooves every serious participant in the interpersonal arena to master.

Personal ethics are probably the most critical variable upon which interpersonal joy and fulfillment can be legitimately based. Understanding the ethical posture of those close to us, not described or articulated but *lived* in their daily lives, is unmatched for reliability as a determinant for a successful relationship with them. Think how many serious arguments turn on how dearly one holds his allegiance to the truth: how responsible one is to adhere to facts and logic; one's understanding of territorial rights and imperatives; one's understanding of mercy and forgiveness; how one assesses and charges for error; what one understands to be the rights and privileges of his neighbor's flesh. Property and sacred symbols are crucial readings which we must record on all others with whom we hope to consort happily and seriously.

In a trial between a rational and an irrational person the irrational person will always win because the rational person is bound to constrict his arguments and hold his rhetoric to the rules and requirements of reason, whereas his irrational opponent in the face of compromise or confrontation with a superior argument may revert to delusion, false premise, false belief and primitive thinking—such that an "A" may be a "non-A," or the same "A" may reside in a different place at the same time. Should one find oneself woefully constricted by having to retaliate one could only reply "We live in different worlds and all likelihood of our compatibility is thereby erased."

12

Responsibility

"Man is the animal who can make promises; can see himself as the one who makes agreements."

—*Nietzsche*

I am frequently called upon by the courts to argue the question of responsibility or to give so-called expert testimony on whether people are responsible for their behavior or whether they are not guilty by reason of insanity (which means that they would be found not culpable for their crimes because they did not have minds that could formulate an intent. They would be found as irresponsible for their behavior as if they were in coma or were an imbecile, or child or mad dog, according to the old literature, where it was decided that children, and the senile, crazy or retarded people could pretty much behave as they liked and be found not responsible for their behavior under the common laws of their Commonwealth). We are not going to talk about responsibility as it relates to crime, but as it relates to all behavior and, specifically, how people understand and decide whether they are or are not responsible for the behavior of others.

Whether or not you have formally considered it, you undoubtedly exercise a rule of thumb when considering whether others are or are not responsible for how they act, feel or think.

We have already briefly asked, "How could they do that to me?" In this chapter we shall ponder the issue of what, if anything, people should be doing with and for each other, and how responsible they are for the consequences of their behavior.

Most simplistically, the behavior of others is minimally two-fold. It is either overt or not. When his fist strikes your nose, wherein you are the object of his act, it is overt. We may then ask, "I wonder why he hit me?" or "I wonder what he meant by that?"

When there is synchrony between the manifest act and the latent motive, life is simple and responsibility is clear. The he who did is the he who meant is the he who is responsible.

But with most folks it is quite different.

The he who did "A" is often the he who meant to do "B"; and the I who does or meant "A" may be experienced by you as the I who did not do "A" or mean to do "B."

This, of course, provides the dilemma for the doer of not knowing how he will be perceived and, secondly, of often not knowing himself the depth or extent of his unconscious intents.

In the first meetings of group therapy sessions, I tell the uncertain members that "here we will observe what people do with each other." Since they are strangers, their manifest neutrality should allow for more acceptance of my interpretations of the actions of other members. The early neutrality, however, soon gives way to old responses as tensions rise and feelings become more intense. Members begin to question whether they deserve to be treated as other members are treating them … they ask if they caused the treatment.

"You have no right to speak to me that way," they protest. Or, "How dare you judge me!" "It wasn't my fault," they argue. "What would you do if someone did/said that to you? Wouldn't you be angry? Disappointed? Wouldn't you want to hurt them back?" Or, pulling back, "I don't have to answer if I don't want to."

They are dealing with the differences between precipitation of stress and of cause … the difference between causing per se and of *causing to make happen*.

There is the conventional notion that "We feel the way we feel and then think and behave accordingly." This puts a low emphasis on choice in our thinking and acting. There is a well-established legal precedent that says, "You take the victim as you find him," ergo if you hold up a store and the proprietor dies of a heart attack in the process, you may be charged with murder despite the fact that he has been in treatment for severe coronary insufficiency for the last 25 years.

There is an extremely interesting legal case now being argued in one of the major appeals courts in which the defendant upon his conviction sued the physician who attended his victim because he believed that the doctor could have saved his victim and, had the victim been saved, the defendant would have only faced the charges of armed robbery. Did the assailant cause the death of the store owner or did he merely effect a stress to which the owner responded and whose response was then controlled by a further set of forces, some of which were voluntary and others which may be termed involuntary, including the possible malpractice of the physician?

But what about the theories of Albert Ellis and Werner Erhard and their cant that "We choose the way we feel on the basis of our ideas."

The question develops great relevance in workmen's compensation claims and other suits against third-party insurance carriers and large corporations or wealthy individuals; and the courts have spoken variously to the complexity which is bolstered by the arguments of conflicted experts.

We shall not resolve this question for you, but we shall do you a greater service which you may at first glance not appreciate. We shall confuse you and provoke you to understand that you act as if you knew the answer to all these questions or—worse yet—you arbitrarily respond to different life circumstances with answers vacillating from one position to another in order to come out as not responsible when anybody feels bad but (aha, and here's the paradox of all paradoxes) fully responsible for people feeling good and thus (yes, you guessed it) deserving of their appreciation and admiration.

To the gremlin who speaks up, "Hey, you can't have it both ways," you reply, "Why not, since nothing matters except the accumulation of pleasure and the diminution or avoidance of pain?"

The final ploy of the maligned to the accusations of an alleged victim is that nothing matters. This allows the accused to sidestep the entire issue. Or the maligned may retort, "It's not that bad. You may feel it's that bad, but your feelings aren't based on my behavior. It couldn't be that bad, even if I knew that action would bother you, because (1) I'm not omnipotent, or (2) you chose to react that way or (3) you're crazy."

Here's another example, from the already-mentioned Dr. Chisholm's Philosophy 101 class:

Your enemy lives alone in a small deserted cottage in a remote section. He is away for several days. You clandestinely secure entrance to his apartment and set up a contraption such that when he opens his front door, a set of levers, weights and pulleys fire a shotgun into the chest of the first person who enters through the locked front door. He enters and dies.

Surely you caused it to happen, even if you hired a paid assassin to construct the murder contraption, and argued that he caused it to happen. But you were the brains behind it. Can you deny responsibility? We are discussing manipulation: the handling of others, the designing of circumstances, motivated by the desire to see others jump, laugh, cry, give up—run toward us with gratitude or away from us with fear and disgust.

To those who argue either that "nothing matters" or that "they chose their response," our reply is *bullshit*! Read no further if nothing matters—if you don't want to be at least partially responsible for the joy of others and, when responsible for their pain, to be responsible to relieve it.[14]

Some people believe that all events are created by cause and effect. This accurately applies to the cause of stones falling to the ground, or of air currents creating hurricane winds. Cause and effect is a very useful and relevant way of looking at phenomena. But does it apply to people?

If an event is caused, then it is not the result of free will. And if it is the result of free will, it has not been caused.

In interpersonal relationships, when is a situation caused and when is it free will? Consider the following example.

You have a friend whom you are very fond of and in whom you've placed your full trust. He betrays you and you feel badly. He asks why you feel so badly and you reply, "Because you betrayed me."

"I don't see the connection," he says. "You chose to feel badly and reacted to my behavior with your choice to feel badly, so I am not the cause of your pain! I simply gave you a stress, to which you responded as you chose to respond."

How would you react to that argument? Would you be put on the defensive by it, or would it infuriate you?

Or, put another way, would you feel entitled to hold him responsible for his actions?

It would seem that your entitlement to hold another responsible depends on whether you have proceeded toward intimacy with him on the basis of consensual agreement or not. Have each of you presented your real selves for the other's viewing, and have those real selves been accurately perceived? If that is so, then have you also agreed on your separate and mutual rights? Did the action that made you feel badly contradict any of your agreed-upon rights?

---

14 A postscript about masochism or repeating pain. It cannot ever be properly argued that someone likes pain. What can be said is that people repeat their mistakes and move toward familiar pain rather than the new and obstensibly more pleasant experiences. When you are in a relationship to a masochist, you are in a no-win box because new behavior is incomprehensible to them. You will struggle ferociously against it; your logic will not be satisfied, you won't believe that you cannot please them, that you can be found guilty when innocent, hostile when kind, dirty when clean. Pray never proclaim your dilemma: "Don't you see how much you're hurting me?" for the pain of their life is already more than they can bear and, by some dreadful magical argument, your pain diminishes their pain and more guilt they don't need!

If his action was to betray a secret you had entrusted him with, was it clearly understood between you that it was, indeed, a secret and that he would respect the privacy of the information?

If you answer yes to all the foregoing, you are now faced with deciding that his betrayal resulted from (1) his intentionally betraying you—in which case he is fully responsible for your reaction or (2) his inability to act as he agreed to ... that, perhaps, he is a compulsive gossip who can't keep anything to himself.

If you decide that the betrayal was intentional, you must then decide how you will respond. You could simply attempt "punishing" him through masochistically "feeling bad." You could retaliate. Or you could decide that he was untrustworthy and not worthy of any further confidences.

If you conclude that, for whatever reason, he was not responsible for his act, you must then certainly decide to no longer take him into your confidence. And you would further have to determine whether or not that person was capable of participating in a good, give-and-take interpersonal relationship.

The issue of responsibility is a crucial one in choosing those with whom we will relate. In this chapter we have raised the questions. Now let us go on to examine how responsibility enters into the interpersonal space.

13

"I Love You"

"Whereas there may be a world where Venus is not the Morning Star, there can be no world where Venus is not Venus."

—*W. Quine*

Nearly 20 years ago an article on love appeared—of all places—in the *New England Journal of Medicine.*

Its contents were delightful for several reasons. First, because it purported to evaluate a subject which had never appeared in the pages of any text course during medical school and, second, because I was at the time wondering about my own inclinations in that regard. Thirdly, I was at that time a newborn Freudian and impressed by Philip Solomon's use of analytic technology for such a project. Over those years I have, through personal and professional experiences, filtered the arguments therein formulated about this profound human feeling and have decided to try my hand at another definition.

I include this because, of all the things that are crucial in the process of understanding significant other people in our lives, no phenomenon would be more crucial for understanding than how to assess the communication "I love you," or how to explain "I love you."

I shall begin by reflecting on a dimension of love so starkly simple that it is a wonder no other author has given voice to its relevance, at least in my readings. It is simply that for the protest, "I love you," there is no consensually validated or general proof.

When one pledges to render a service, promises to accomplish an errand and does as agreed, the result may be acknowledged as follows: "That was nice of you *to do* that which surely reveals that you care and have an interest in me." If the other replies, "Yes and more, I love you also," we may rejoice in good faith, believing that if spoken then it is so. Herein, of course, lies the rub. If spoken, is it indeed so?

Let us imagine two young friends in the latter days of their courtship. Both feel comfortable in asserting "I like you very much," and both seem to know that however lovely that may be, there is a serious and significant psychological leap from such a statement and position stand to the statement, "I love you."

My own view is that the intrinsically disruptive and delaying issue here is that, somehow, *liking* is a situational verb. It is a playing statement for the here and now, whereas the phenomenon of *loving* for many is part of the quest for defining one's identity and seems to absorb into its meaning concepts of essence and endurance. When someone says, "I love you," what he seems to mean, as I construe it, is that "Whoever I am, that essential 'I' is open to you for a promised long time."

Thereby, one reciprocal dimension of its meaning is vulnerability—for it is a denuding statement insofar as it identifies one's underlying essence from the situational, marginal or superficial parts of one's personality. Whereas loving may appear to be derived from one's essential values, paradoxically it may be the mechanism whereby we know that we have such essential values.

Just as in stress we may find unknown or unused resources, so in loving may we find a previously unknown dimension of our existence. If we falsely define the other as the *only* other who can find this trait in us (as is too frequently the case) then unhappily and illogically we may be forced to say in loss, "Without you I am without my essential self—I am nothing."

Charlie, the law student from New Rochelle, in his blue oxford button-down shirt, driving his '59 Triumph, living in Cambridge or Ann Arbor, whose father owns the Cindy's Sportswear Shops can, today, with a little encouragement, easily take his pants off with most coeds. But if loving means daring to find our essential selves, then for this enterprise he is less courageous.

Come briefly with me to a fairy tale to understand why I talk of dare and courage. You recall that it was not that Rumplestiltskin didn't know what his name was; it was when others knew what it was that he would explode. In our quest to understand love, what seems to be the crucial issue is that we entrust to another the specific privilege of *entry into a space in which some personal characteristic previously beheld only marginally (if at all) by us is now exposed for validation.*

Never saying "I love you" means never knowing whether another person can experience it as true. But is this sufficient? Hardly so, for it speaks of love in that casual unthinking way which allows it to be a possibility for all who have the vocabulary. If love is only entry into our inner nakedness, it is more passive than I believe is appropriate.

Love is, then, more than permission to come in and look and feel me. It is complemented by the suggestion or promise that something really valuable and pleasurable will occur.

For some, "I love you" means "Come into my private place and validate my essential self in a positive way, for which I shall respond with joy and gratitude by exclaiming 'I love you.' You then, so moved, may experiment with a like invitation and I will reciprocate by validating your inner self such as will allow you to joyfully reply, 'And I love you too!'"

Infatuation and Delusion

What is lacking in this? Let us begin by returning to Philip Solomon's essay. He talks about the idea of infatuation or romantic love as follows:

"A new phenomenon may now appear: the boy 'falls in love' with a girl. What happens? The girl regards him as the very same hero he has been wishing he were! He accepts her verdict and adores her for it. The affair is reciprocal: she in turn sees in his eyes the girl she has been yearning to be, and they dote on one another. A crossed identification takes place. Regarding their judgments of one another, each adopts that of the other—and gladly, since it happens to correspond to what is wished for but despaired of in each. The result is an infatuation, characterized by marked over-evaluation of the love object. The boy thinks he loves the girl. What he loves is the idealized version of himself that she sees in him. When he is with her he can believe that he *is* the idealized self that he wishes he were. This phenomenon of infatuation is the basis for romantic love."

It is evident that several conditions are necessary before it can come about:

1. There must be an appreciable discrepancy between the actual self and the ideal self. In societies where ambition and competition are at a minimum, romantic love is virtually unknown. In the present highly competitive modern civilization, full of ever-increasing standards and further-reaching goals, romantic infatuation, with its sequels of poorly chosen marriages, divorce and broken homes, has become a serious problem.

2. Maturity of personality must be lacking.

3. The sense of reality must be capable of being put in abeyance.

4. The infatuation must be reciprocal. Since being loved is the essence of infatuation, it cannot occur unilaterally.

5. The girl (or other) must possess some attributes in reality that the boy (or other) finds attractive; otherwise he could not value her judgment or identify himself with her...

In romantic love, saying "I love you" is in a sense a proposition of *folie à deux*. It means trading and sharing the delusions of my view of me and your view of you.

Our view of loving is precisely the opposite. It is using love as a way to validate one's essential capability for loving and being loved for one's truth.

"I love you" is then taking a chance that moving one step closer for a more careful look will be more interesting than staying away, that focusing a new higher magnification lens onto an observing other is worth the chance. Insofar as this occurs it opens the possibility for the next step which reads as follows:

"Having been close and seen, I would now like to mix myself with you in that supreme experiment in which oneness is forever taken and I am thenceforward of us." It is a mini-Hegelian drama. It is the synthesis of two I's. Love is the consummation of the synthesis of those dialectical others: I and I, who once were selfish, are now we. To love someone is the invitation to mix with them and thenceforward to know yourself only as not part of the other but part of the new "we" which is more than each and as much as those two can discover. Love then, when uttered by each, is an "I want to" statement.

What advice can we provide our young and old lovers on the basis of this explanation? The first piece of advice is the clarification that it is a gamble. The second is that before it can be realistically comprehended, that excruciatingly complex awareness needs to be conveyed about how much different a "we" is from two "I's." The loss of "I" must clearly be understood and comprehended. By definition you will never be the same again so long as you are in a reciprocal love.

And now another point. What of the reversibility of the process? Can we extricate ourselves from such a union ... collect our now disbursed "I" parts from the mixture of us and depart, or are we irreversibly set?

The concepts of dilute versus enrich may prove helpful. Can one self dilute another and, if so, is that okay? Can a rather mild person decompress an exaggerated hyperactive one in the mixture of "us"?

Couples in love are doing themselves a great injustice if they do not apply reason to their union. The state of love has many of the characteristics of the political state and demands laws to secure the ethical contract. Like all ethical agreements, it can only occur between reasonable citizens.

Who Can Love?

Children cannot reason its worth and therefore cannot love each other or their parents.

We are now trespassing into extraordinary radical proclamations. We hope, however, that in stealing this privilege from children and the immature, we consign to love a value superior to the one presently bandied about. We are driven to this viewpoint as we proceed to define love as a diadic experience—not so much to deprive some of the rights and privileges of loving but to emphasize that the *worth* of love is *the sole judgment of the loved* and that part of the validating process of its truth and worth is *to sort it from infatuation and dependency*.

Now perhaps children can do this but we prefer another verb for them. Before this chapter is over we shall have a delightful new term for them.

We adore children. They snuggle and cling to us, to our mutual delight. But there is no ethical contract that can be appropriately drawn by them. You must be an advanced player in the game of human intercourse to either love or be loved, and the best matches are between those who can do both. You can't do one, *by definition*, without being able to do the other. Being loved is the dessert that is deserved by those who can love. It does not follow that because you can love you will be loved, but it sure helps. For you are loveable for your loving traits. Also though one may feel loved it does not follow that he is loved. In fact, in cleaning up the overuse and sloppy use of this term we must refine our receptors so that only true love will be felt as love, for only when properly felt does it exist.

Thus it would follow that one could never say "I love you" until the loved one were to respond "I feel loved." The receipt of love validates it. "I love you" has no intrinsic cash value for you: to indulge in the nonsense that it does allow us to use the experience of loving others in a masturbatory fashion. This metaphor may appear too crude, but I believe it uniquely comprehends the issue. For have we not heard both male and female partners wonder whether the physical expression of their presumed love relationship was in fact masturbation? And if we call sexual intercourse in some instances love making, may we not likewise deign to call some loving masturbation? What we are trying to do here is find verbs in the instance of loving and understand which derive their meaning only upon receipt.

Let's approach the issue with several other examples:

"I hurt you" has no meaning without the reciprocal notion of "You are hurting because of what I do to you and you must validate the hurt before it can be said that I have hurt you," whereas "I pour water on you" clearly may be true whether you validate it or not. Harry Stack Sullivan built an entire discipline of interpersonal psychiatry upon this notion of "consensual validation." You may say—even protest—that you love and understand me; but it is only when I affirm that I feel loved and understood that you are validated for having loved and understood me.

When confronted by a spouse or partner who would say, "Charlie, I don't feel you love me anymore," it makes no sense to argue, "Yes, I do." What makes sense is to wonder what she means by that or more adequately to ask, "I wonder why my feelings and ideas, which left me as love and understanding, have arrived misperceived and ineffectual toward the goal of calling forth her receipt of my love and awareness of her?"

Two clear areas to pursue the resolution of this dilemma are:

1. What is the matter with you that you don't experience me as loving and understanding you?

2. What is the matter with me that I can't get you to experience me as loving and understanding?

14

Love and Sex

"It's terrible to see how a single unclear idea lurking in a young man's head like an obstruction of inert matter in an artery—hindering the nutrition of the brain—condemns its victim to pine away in the fullness of his individual vigor .... Many a man had cherished for years some vague shadow of an idea too meaningless to be positively false. He nevertheless passionately loved it ... leaving all other occupation for its sake ... flesh of his flesh ... bond of his bond."

—*C. S. Peirce*

Sex Play

There is an interesting Lenny Bruce sketch in which he satirizes that desperate moment of inquiry when many males ask, "Was that good for you? Did you come?"

Though otherwise disadvantaged by culture and biology, in her physically always-ready state for intercourse and with her less apparent increased physiology for orgasm, women have a weaponry system for significant counterbalance to at least some male prerogatives and arrogance.

As Mr. Bruce mocks the dialogue by crescendoing the inquiry and adding melody to it—he touches a vitally important issue in male/female gamesmanship.

How has it come to pass that the male is so preoccupied with female orgasm and so unmoved by clearly supportive and affirming statements such as "That was lovely," and "I really enjoyed it." Why his insistence, "Did you come?"

Now to be sure, partners do have a legitimate curiosity about whether orgasm was achieved and they should be attentive to techniques suggested by the other to facilitate orgasm. But in fact each partner is responsible for his own climax and the question of male preoccupation with the climax of his female partners is an extremely interesting one.

Another view of this may be seen in the following:

Some years after treating a college sophomore I received his manuscript which had just won a national competition for young playwrights. It recounted one of our sessions in which he had a fantasy about a mistress with two vaginas: one for "fucking" the other for "making love." In the first act there is a very poignant scene when one of her lovers, in the delightful afterglow of a mutually exciting and climactic sexual experience, inquires first playfully but shortly thereafter in deadly seriousness, "Which one?"

As the sequence progresses he becomes progressively hostile believing that he has been duped and exploited, for while convinced that he was making love he now realizes that he had only been fucking.

This confusion derives from the American cultural folkway that sexual intercourse should occur in the context of a significant and meaningful interpersonal relationship. Well, that sounds fine if you believe that 14-, 15- and 16-year-old adolescents can and do in fact have such quality unions. What rather occurs is that in order to rationalize an already existing experience of sexual intercourse they *post hoc* conclude that they have such a deep and abiding commitment to one another in order to *justify* their performance.

The charade is a tragic one, for it disallows that crucial awareness that by choice and mutual agreement individuals may have sexual play as well as other games. Thanks to Walter Lippmann's beautiful essay on this very subject we know how it came to be otherwise. Only when sex and procreation became scientifically separated for the masses (i.e., almost universal birth control information and availability) did it occur to the average man or woman that it could be otherwise. And so the age of sex play for adults is upon us. Playing with random partners in pursuit of a final special spouse allows the valuable opportunity to not confuse sexual compatibility with personal worth. However, it does not follow that sexual fidelity is now an outmoded value.

The analogy of enriching or diluting a broth seems to be an applicable metaphor. And while we are using figures of speech let's not forget that a marriage is no more nor less than the idea of the couple so wed. It has the potential (if you are Hegelian) as do all ideas, of being more than each of the mere individual persons who have created and conceptualized their union.

People who have a sense of private personal places and parts seem more disposed to the fidelity constraint than those who do not.

The rationale seems elemental and poetically primitive. Given our mammalian heritage we are forever drawn to those primary moments of infant-with protecting-adult. Should we, any of us, be so fortunate as to secure and preserve a contemporary relationship which provides for each partner re-enactments of those crucial moments of our history, is it any wonder that we are symbolically devastated when that space is invaded by rivals?

I guess what we're aiming at here is that no one is ever a naked "I." At the minimum he is an I/there and in a progressive awareness of the there places in which special others reside do we more honestly get to know them. And, at those moments when we know where they are by being there with them may they truly be said to light up our life. Thus it may become not "There but for the grace of God go I," but "There in the grace of caring go we."

Sex and Love

Whatever else we may have learned from dear "Ziggy" Freud, surely we are in his debt for having articulated a formulation of human sexuality that has provoked us to think more profoundly and intelligently about it than had previously been the case. No aspect of another person's life is more worthy of our study in understanding him than his sexuality. With Freud as our teacher of reference, let us examine his paper *Three Contributions Toward the Theory of Human Sexuality*. In this article, Freud announced that: whereas urges to have relief of sexual tension were genetic and biological, method to accomplish this and person/partner chosen, were cultural.

How provocative to consider that all we require for a physically sexually satisfying experience is a learned partner and method; and that all that is *inherent* is a biological pressure and craving for relief of tension in the various erotic places of our anatomy which have that physiological capability for the build-up of tension and climactic relief. The most current restatement of this awareness is provided in the Masters and Johnson and Shere Hite research reports, where it is established by all the technology available in their laboratory and questionnaire methods that quantitatively superior physiological climaxes are achieved when the stimulator is self, and the method is manual, with or without mechanical assistance, i.e., masturbation!

Consider the impact of this experimental finding. It basically advises us that when body/carnal pleasure is desired, masturbation is more likely to elicit a higher physiological state of climax and relief than is probable through interpersonal sexual intercourse. Then why choose the interpersonal method? The answer is related to who is the "I" who lives in or has that body, and the learned likelihood that a more enjoyable synthesis can be negotiated when language, empathy, caring and tenderness are culturally wed to the carnal pleasures of the organs themselves. To the extent that others can be and are understood, these latter possibilities enhance.

Sexual delight can be enriched by grafting love and caring upon it. Conversely, fear and loathing can deny one's anatomical potential. Thus the crude and belligerent formulation of the male chauvinist is repudiated when in situations of rape he urges the partner to "enjoy it, because it's going to happen anyway." We have known interrogating police officers to put rape victims through more humiliating experiences than the rape, by inquiring of them whether or not they "enjoyed" the experience insofar as a pleasure organ of the body has been stimulated. Such a base inquiry derives from primitive logic, misperceiving that learning and culture can and do declare their own limits on body function, and that nurture can and does attain dominance over "natural" animal instincts.

In questing to understand someone else for a change, we cannot presume that their sexual organs are intrinsically pleasure territories and relate to them in terms of the number of nerve endings residing there, nor with a technology for stimulating them. In looking for sexual pleasure with a partner one should have a full awareness of how his or her body pleasure potentials have been altered by cultural contradictions. We must inquire into our partner's messages regarding method, technique, aim, style, mode, time, etc.—otherwise the sexual experience will be not only not pleasurable, it will be exploitive. Whereas this pertains to both men and women, it is generally more crucial that the male understand his female partner in this respect. He must appreciate what quality of synthesis she has experienced between affirmation of erotic zones of pleasure and cultural sanctions and admonitions concerning technique, aim, style and frequency.

The female partner must comprehend that the sexual life of her partner is less encumbered by such cultural factors—indeed he is charged to be more primitive and naked of restraint in giving expression to his sexual needs and finding relief for his sexual tensions. And she should also recognize that he has probably paid dearly for this somewhat mixed blessing of freedom, for having forsaken tenderness in his youth he may have won impotence in his middle age.

A paradox here is the higher capability of the female for on-going sexual climax as opposed to male sexuality which is conspicuous for cresting, climax and then a return to a neutral state of sexual inefficiency with a latent or lag phase before renewed interest or capability. There are astounding figures to document this: women whose graphs of sexual climax show upwards of 50 to 100 physiological orgasms on a regular and repeatable basis. This paradox is rendered more dramatic when we read of so many women who, in their entire lives as active sexual spouses, may have few if any orgasms—as contrasted with the almost universal likelihood of a single male climax in most all sexual encounters.

When these facts are clarified, why is the newly educated female not more inclined to seek out repetitive climaxes in the light of her higher capability? Why is she not the pursuer more often than the pursued? Why in the marriage counseling chambers across the country is it not she who is more regularly coming in to protest frustration and disappointment in her intimate life—why is it rather the husband whose sexual capability is physiologically far less efficient, who is the chronic complainer in sexual incompatibility matters?

Even before husbands gain this new awareness of the female orgasmic potential, when they define their partners or spouses as having passive sexuality, they ask: "Why is this withheld? Why is allowing entry such a chore of relating?" The answer is self-evident: cultural permission and the perennial battle of the sexes. It appears that women were willing to forsake their physiological sexual endowments by essentially repudiating their anatomy to secure at least one zone of mastery over the prejudice of chauvinist males. Men's own mythology about female orgasm in the final analysis caused them probably more travail than to their women, who at least were spared more procreation than their already overburdened uteruses could accommodate.

The new sanctions of the 1960s cannot erase the nurturing of the 1940s— which casts its shadow well across the present. So let's pause to explore this nurture process. Reflect with me for a while on the cultural tasks facing the infant male on his way to maturity.

He begins in intimate relationship to the female breasts, lips, buttocks, genitalia; comes to experience this female as his rightful place for pleasure and intimacy. He moves through a latency and pre-adolescent phase where chums, buddies and boyfriends are the special others to share with and where female compatibility reveals his "sissy" traits; where girlfriends make him less acceptable to his peer group than boyfriends, and relationships to them less manly; but he then is biologically thrust into adolescence where warmth to buddies and chums is fey and if (as a heterosexual) he is not intimate with women—does not prefer a date with his girlfriend to a game of chess with his boyfriend—then he is perverse and out of step. So, however circuitously, he comes to rest sexually with his primary female objects.

Women, on the other hand, born of the same women as their brothers, are likewise reared in proximity to their mother's breasts, hips, lips, thighs and cheeks, and likewise move into their pre-adolescent and latency years persistently close to other women—playing house, with dolls, going to pajama parties, etc. Then somewhat abruptly during adolescence they are expected to make radical alterations in choice of others for conversation, intimacy and friendship, and must now become spouses, friends and sexual partners of men. One can teach in Sociology 101 that there should be a better way ... and there probably is .... but for now insofar as these facts prevail, we as adults must try to relate to other similarly reared adults.

There would be no better way to undo these impediments than to secure an empathy and understanding for our rearing and learned sexual differences. We must understand how the heterosexual partner feels, is and has became before it is feasible for us to negotiate anything but a carnal communion!

Thus in understanding someone else it would be a primary task to appreciate that someone else is not a person with a sexuality which operates separately, but a psychobiological totality and that however primitive our formula may be, no one can truly relate to anyone without a working theory of their mind–body relationships—especially in the specific quest for sexual compatibility.

One of the most necessary dimensions of personal maturity is the articulation and definition of as many of our underlying premises and theories for our judgments as we can come upon. I am particularly persuaded that in the area of human sexuality it behooves us to make a thorough inquiry as to how the other person sees, experiences and fits into their body—without cluttering our quest with pre-judgment.

While we highlight this issue by speaking of sexuality there are innumerable other instances where insight into another's mind/body relationships can be extremely helpful in understanding them. Whether it's wanting or not wanting to be touched while sleeping, sharing a toothbrush, accepting nudity, growing a beard or shaving under the arms, it cannot be exaggerated that as one knows the needs and attitudes which another has about their body, the more likely the chance of securing a successful relationship with that person.

The introductory paragraphs of this chapter almost seem to provoke the question, "Well in that case why have sex with another person at all?" Note that I didn't say, "Why have sex?" but "Why with another person?" For we noted that thanks to Masters and Johnson we are assured of having a more satisfying psychochemical phenomenon with masturbation (with or without vibrators with their new Teflon edges and low, medium and high speed ranges) than with another human. Thus no argument could be supported which says that sex with another person is a physically, chemically or physiologically better experience than sex alone or with an object.

The issue is that preference for another person over the self is psychological—not genetic, not biological, not procreative. The discussion of choice or preference for another person of the same or opposite sex will be deferred. However, the general answer, "person over object or self," is no more profound than to state that coupling biological satisfaction with interpersonal satisfactions potentiates the former.

Our inclination toward interpersonal sexuality is the prospect of melding that biological experience with friendship, loving, shared history, working, playing and laughing. As these dimensions of culture insinuate into the interbiological experience they grade it, color it, shade it and render it more pleasurable. The question, "Why have sex with another person?" may be extended to considerations of why sleep, walk, talk, play, see a movie or eat a meal with someone else rather than alone; and the answer is the same.

As Lou Andreas-Salome stated so beautifully: "Persons represent more to us than we ourselves do to the external world and we only touch by a backward turn; only in personal relations do we find direction."

It is in the interpersonal sphere that we are, by culture, directed to experience a higher sense of satisfaction than in the solitary state.

Whatever your formulation as to why, it does occur that for most people it is more fun to be with others than alone and *a very important reason for understanding others is to facilitate such intimacy.*

15

Responsibility and Love

*"Much misconstruction and bitterness are spared to
him who thinks naturally upon what he owes to others
rather than what he ought expect from them."*

—*Madame Guizot*

Let us distinguish between love and like. How often we hear our friends comment upon their relationships with others, saying that the other person is loved but not liked, or liked but not loved. Now whereas the possibilities are, of course, mathematically quite simple—another person may be liked and loved, liked but not loved—loved but not liked is not a real or viable possibility.

We cannot accept that a person whom we love does not possess those traits and virtues that renders them either additionally likeable or preconditionally loveable as well. Let's consider this in terms of action and performance.

A person who does the things we love may be loved, and by the same token the person who does the things we like may be liked. Therefore we may inquire what things/acts do we love and what things/acts do we like? Is there a mere quantitative difference? No. The difference seems to be qualitative. "I love" a hot bath; lobster, fisherman-style; truth; my mother or my mistress, is clearly different from "I like" those same things or persons.

Are there some experiences which are so special that "like" is inadequate to their extraordinariness? "How was your trip to the moon, Mr. Astronaut?" "Oh, I liked it."

Is "chemistry" more a love phenomenon than a like trait? Are there things we might do for someone we loved that we would not likely do for someone we liked and vice versa? Are some things we would expect from someone who professed to love us more so than from someone who liked us? How does sexuality apply? How does age difference apply? In understanding other people it is crucial that the distinctions between like and love be given a full analysis, and in the process we must consider the issue of infatuation.

How often have we observed in novels or movies the object of a love protest retorting, "But you hardly know me, Charlies." "That doesn't matter," he insists,

"I love you." In saying, "You hardly know me," our respondent has conveyed an inherent awareness that "not knowing me" means not having enough information to even like me, let alone love me. People seem to know that whereas one may intuitively wish and desire to leap to love, that one must instead traverse step by step the pathway of caring for, liking, respecting and admiring.

Now it can be argued that it does occur otherwise and that, fortuitously after a love protest (however unrealistic), care, admiration and respect follow. For those so blessed, nature and destiny have truly smiled but when so, it is luck not truth which has prevailed.

There is the demand that these other attitudes be present before we acknowledge a love contract. This may be better understood if we inquire into that process wherein, from a mix of purported love, like, admiration and respect, the latter three fade yet the individual continues to protest the endurance of his love. How can we realistically allow this to exist as a proper occurrence? Our answer is that we cannot and it therefore becomes us as loved ones to demand, prior to accepting such a protest, that a legitimate series of conditions occur which mandate its proper use, and the absence of which can contradict it.

The semanticists and culture passers of our society have allowed us to persist with a sloppy irreverent use of the crucial verb "to love" in our vocabulary. Without belaboring the whys or wherefores of this, this is meant to relieve those who read it of having to play the love game without a proper set of rules and regulations.

Forgive us if we do appear callous to the young poets and nymphets whose notions of "I'm nothing without you," etc., unfortunately move us not the slightest. What we hope to accomplish by this chapter is to tell you that misunderstanding the experience of your own love for someone else, or someone else's love for you, is possibly and in fact likely to be the most tragic misunderstanding it would ever be your misfortune to accomplish. Accordingly you cannot afford to play love games; you can only afford to play like games and sex games.

What has happened however is this: We have advised and acculturated our young people to believe that coincident with the ability to have sexual relationship is the ability to have a loving relationship. We have suggested that in order to be properly expressed sexually, one must be in a loving relationship. What has then quite predictably occurred is that, in a pathetic effort to validate their sexuality, young men and women have been duped into believing that they are in love. This chapter contradicts that lie, hopefully forever, for its readers, and argues that love is for adults ... that it is only adults who can be in love with each other. That whereas children and adolescents may play infatuation and sex games—the game of love requires certification, apprenticeship and rites of initiation. And that only in consummation of these is "I love you" a credible, responsible and reliable statement. It is surely possible to say to another, "I hear you say that you love me and perhaps you believe that you love me but you don't have the credentials nor have you met the criteria that warrants my accepting it."

Let me cite an analogous situation wherein one might protest, "I can lift a thousand pounds." Another might retort that, "If you can lift a thousand pounds, prove it." Just as one would then accordingly have to demonstrate the musculature, coordination and training to lift 1,000 lb., so would one have to demonstrate the psychological musculature and discipline to warrant the challenge, "I love you." In fact, the one so accosted may reply, "Who taught you to love? What experiences of love have you received that equips you to give what you have received?" This is an extraordinarily important point. The credentials of all lovers should contain evidence that they have themselves experienced the love of other adults, with inventories and signed receipts for such experiences.

"How crass," you may respond. "How banal to put your lover through such an obstacle course." Our reply is simply that when involved in the experience of loving, the consequences are too grave for the participation of beginners. What all too often occurs in such a process is the awareness that the other's statement, "I love you" turns out to be more a statement about him than you.

We would prefer, when someone tells us that they love us, that who we are and how we are chosen had been a carefully and judiciously considered judgment on their part. But the fact of the matter is that too often in saying, "I love you," the speaker is deeply if not pathologically preoccupied with the "I" than the "you."

Epilogue

OK, so now you're there. You have (1) disencumbered yourself from resistances, reluctances, fears, doubts and blocks, et al., to the proper perception of those others who you now understand better because of this.

Likewise (2) you have new skills quite aside from the above, new techniques, new modes of listening, a new style of empathy—you know much more about how the other guy feels or ticks.

OK—is that it? Well, perhaps for some there will be a joy in knowing the *more* that you know—the pleasure of achievement—mastery of a new craft. The once called "aha" experience is now yours.

Our view, however, is that these skills and new truths run through your own existence like a plow that turns and furrows the earth of you, so that you are re-discovered and re-motivated to do something about "it," and this doing may be defined in the interpersonal sphere as trimodal:

1. You will resolve conflicts and move closer to those understood others. You will extend your intimate range or, perhaps better stated, you will find a place for remote others in your intermediate and intimate sphere.

2. You will acknowledge irreconcilable differences and allow the transfer of current intimates to more remote assignments in your world.

3. You will develop a new awareness of the often oversimplified notion of give and take. You will no longer be frustrated by the apparent imbalances of give and take but will understand that giving is more aptly identified by your new awareness of the resources of the giver than by the weight and dimension of his gift, and so you will conversely re-adjust your own needs to this new truth.

4. You will have a new appreciation of the complex interplay of sex, love and marriage as you watch others struggle with their views of the proper linkage between these experiences, i.e.,

    -those who sex without love and/or marriage,
    -those who love without sex and/or marriage,
    -those who are married without love and/or sex,
    -those who cannot sex without love,
    -those who cannot love without sex.

You will experience in yourself a new awareness of how you are reciprocal to them. You will emancipate yourself from life's probably most seductive and potentially deceitful word game.

5. You will for perhaps the first time in your life have understood how beholden you have been too naive and false premise beliefs about the nature of yourself and those others about you, and the things you exchange with them.

    Mind-body dichotomous formulations will no longer limit your argument . . . *ego* horsemen riding *id* stallions will phase to notions of centaurs. Knowing people in their places shall have become the operant variable in your new perceptions—not wondering about their non-existent minds or personalities.

6. The creation of a relationship through your ideas about that relationship shall emerge as a more noble enterprise than understanding yourself alone.

    "What are we now doing with each other?" and "How may we otherwise interact?" shall have become the essential questions of your existence as you see (as Harry S. Sullivan taught us 50 years ago) that psychiatry is the study of pathological relationships later revised to be people communicating ineptly.

7. You will have a new view of responsibility. You will no longer indulge yourself with either/or answers to complex questions. Ideas of "both" and "neither" will become equally relevant to questions of why people did what they did and you will now understand that the "I" who did is the "I" who is responsible. But you shall now wonder about the continuity of selves in time: you will want a better way of knowing if this man in the defendant's chair is the *same* man who was the perpetrator of the crime for which he is now being tried.

    You will thus see that malice of forethought, meanness and vengefulness are not mutually exclusive of psychosis, i.e., paranoid thinking or irresistible impulse.

8. You will be less quick to talk of "sickness" in our society or in others and more likely to apply the truth that, just because it was discovered by psychiatrists and used to alter the behavior of their patients, does not mean that all behavior which we want altered need be tended by those same practitioners.

9. You will have learned how important models are to our understanding of others and ourselves. You will have a new appreciation

of metaphor and parable in understanding the human condition. You will now see what E. E. Cummings meant when he said, "Always the more beautiful answer for him who asks the more beautiful question."

Your questions about yourself will be more profound for you will have seen so much more to wonder at as you have seen your image reflected off the mirror of those who you have studied and understood.

10. You will have a new regard for the concept of survival in the human condition. You will have a vocabulary not only for the mechanisms of defense but also for the mechanisms of offense. You will see that it is not just simply that people bring out the worst in each other very often, but more precisely that when we believe our survival is threatened we proceed to life and death solutions—however distorted our original judgment may be to neutral observers.

11. You will have developed a new regard for paradox: if my kindness is killing you then I, as killer, will persist in being kind.

12. You will understand how often, in the ostensible struggle and quest for the truth, that the failure of the adversary becomes the prevailing issue. Not "I am right," but "You are wrong!" That is, that you will fail in changing me because it is more important to you that I be wrong than that I become otherwise in the service of us or truth.

13. Most interestingly you will have an extraordinary new and rich vocabulary for that idea of "us."

14. You will have learned that ideas of "best" are more often better replaced by ideas of "least disadvantageous alternative."

15. You will have a better idea of what "that" means in statements:

> It's not "that" bad.
>
> or
>
> It is "that" bad . . . such that I must now do x, y or z.

You will see that when you must do this because it is "that" bad you are in a tautological bind and that your logic is spurious, i.e., "In order to do this, I must know/believe that it is 'that bad.'"

16. You will have a new understanding of the folly and paralysis of the wayfarer stuck between two goods because he cannot decide which is best.

Socrates: "And are you still in labour and travail, my dear friend, or have you brought forth all that you have to say about knowledge to the birth?"

Theatetus: "I am sure, Socrates, that you have elicited more from me, a good deal more than ever was in me."

Socrates: "But, if, Theatetus, you should ever conceive afresh you will be all the better for the present investigation . . .. You will be soberer and humbler and gentler to other men and will be too modest to fancy that you know what you do not know . . . I can no further go."

• • •

Alfred Fireman, MD
September 15, 1930 – October 13, 1998

Resume / Curriculum Vitae

35 years of clinical psychiatric practice

Undergraduate and Professional Education
Brown University, A.B. Cum Laude, Phi Beta Kappa, 9/48–6/52
Tufts University Medical School, M.D. Pfizer Scholarship, 9/52–6/56

Post Doctoral Training and Experience
Rotating Internship, King's County Hospital, Brooklyn, NY, 7/56–6/57
Resident in Psychiatry, Boston V.A. Hospital, 7/57–6/58
Resident in Psychiatry, Boston University Hospital, 7/58–6/59 and 7/61–6/62
Fellowship, National Endowment for the Humanities, University of Texas,
    Medical Ethics, Summer, 1976
Brown University Summer College, International Relations, 1980
Fellow, Kennedy Institute for Ethics, Georgetown, DC, Summer, 1981
Annual certified continuing medical education credits for 34 years (primarily in forensic
    psychiatry)

Certifications and Licensure
Diplomate of the National Board of Medical Examiners, 7/57
Diplomate of the American Board of Psychiatry and Neurology, 10/63
Medical Licensure: MA #26523, 1/61, and RI #3561, 6/62, inactive; FL #17915, 8/71,
    active (with certified CME credits until recertification due in 2001 (primarily secured
    in forensic psychiatry)

Prior Practice, Consultantships, Community Service, and Hospital Staff Appointments
Rhode Island, 1962–1971:
Staff Psychiatrist, Butler Hospital; Clinical Director, East Bay Counseling Center;
    Chairman, Mayor's Committee for Community Mental Health Planning; Senior
    Board Member, Community Mental Health Clinic; Planned Parenthood; Division of
    Vocational Rehabilitation; Model Cities Juvenile Delinquency Project; Marathon Drug
    Rehabilitation House; Major Corporate Personnel Departments; Tunisia Peace Corps
    Project; U.S. Department of Defense (Industrial Security Clearance Office), U.S. Navy
    War College

Florida, 1972–1996:
Psychiatrist-in-chief, University of South Florida Student Health and Counseling Cen-
    ter; Director, Alcohol and Drug Rehab Unit, Bay Pines V.A. Hospital; Private Practice
    of General Psychiatry with consultantships to Alzheimer's Information and Family
    Resource Center; The Institute for Rational Living (and their several sales promotion
    seminars); Agenda Marketing (an international timeshare organization); U.S. Coast
    Guard Air Station Dispensary and Pinellas County Homeless Center

Hospital Staff Appointments:
Psychiatric (1972–1996): Medfield, Horizon, Fairwinds
General (1972–1996): Largo Medical Center, Morton Plant, St. Petersburg General,
   Palms of Pasadena

Forensic Sub Specialization
Research Assistant for mentally disordered sex offenders, Walpole and Bridgewater State
   Prisons, MA, 1958
Residency Rotation, Boston University Law Medicine Institute, 1959
Eastern Regional Consultant to APA Committee on Corrections, 1959–61
Lieutenant, U.S. Navy, Chief Psychiatrist, Maximum Security Prison, Portsmouth, NH,
   1959–61
Director, Parole Clinic, Massachusetts Department of Mental Health, 1962
Consultant, Rhode Island Public Defender's and District Attorney's Offices, 1963–71
Forensic expert witness in State and Federal Courts of RI, NH, MA, and FL, from 1963
   to present
Consultant psychiatrist, Pinellas County Jail, 1975–83
Consultant, Florida Department of Professional Regulation, 1987–90

Publications and Presentations – Forensic
"Pre-Acute Crime Milieu," *Archives of Criminal Psychodynamics*, Spring, 1961. Abstracted
   in *Digest of Neurology and Psychiatry*, Hartford Institute

"A Psychiatrist Takes the Stand," *American Journal of Corrections*, 3/62

Leader, Rhode Island Conference of Social Work Annual Institutes, "Problems of
   Responsibility in Criminal Behavior," 1963 and 1964

"A Study of the Interaction Between Prisoners and Guards," *American Journal of Corrections*, Jan./Feb., 1963

"Problems of Criminal Responsibility," *Rhode Island Medical Journal*, 1/63. Abstracted in
   Excepta Medica Psychiatra

Discussant, John McDonald's paper, "The Threat to Kill," APA Meeting, St. Louis, MO,
   5/63

Editorial Viewpoint in *Florida Bar Journal*, "Dangerousness is Not a Medical Issue," Vol.
   51, No. 3, 3/77

"Confessions of a Forensic Psychiatrist," read at the 9th Annual Meeting of the American Academy of Psychiatry and the Law, Montreal, Canada, 10/78, and published in
   the *American Journal of Forensic Psychiatry*, Vol. 1, No. 2, 2/79

"On the Use of Psychotropics in a County Jail," Workshop at AMA, Meetings on Correction Medicine,Chicago, IL, 10/80

CLE Symposium: "Challenging Psychiatric and Psychological Testimony," Atlanta, GA, 2/81; New Orleans, LA, 2/81; Pensacola, FL, 3/81 (primary speaker)

Producer/Director of 90-minute video documentary on the interface between crime and mental illness as portrayed in 11 clinical interviews with selected inmates at the Pinellas County Jail, presented at the American Medical Association Fifth National Conference on Medical Care and Health Services in Correctional Institutions, Chicago, IL, 10/81; revised and presented to the Society of Health and Human Values Southern Regional Meeting, Charleston, SC, Medical School, Spring, 1982

"A Study of the Health Care Services at the Pinellas County Jail, Clearwater, Florida," presented on contract to Pinellas County Commissioners, 2/83

"Update Report on the Use of Psychotropics in a Jail and Prison Setting," Second World Congress of Prison Health Care, Ottawa, Canada, 8/83

"A Study of the Relationship Between Crime and Mental Illness," presented at the American College of Forensic Psychiatry Annual Meeting, Sanibel Island, FL, 4/86

"Using Medical Expert Witnesses," CLER Lecture Program, Tampa and Miami, FL, 11/92

Publications and Presentations – Other
"An Experiment in Community Education," *Rhode Island Medical Journal*, 1/65. Read at APA Divisional Meeting, Philadelphia, PA, 11/65

"Socrates and Psychotherapy," read at APA Meeting, Atlantic City, NY, 5/66. Published in *Journal of Existential Psychiatry*, 1966. Abstracted in *Psychiatric Spectator*, Sandoz, 1966

"Industrial Psychiatry," Eleventh Annual University of Rhode Island Safety Institute, 1968 Panel Moderator, American Ontoanalytic Meeting, Boston, MA, 5/68; topic: "Existential Psychiatry." Discussants: A. Maslow, William Barrett, Stanley Diamond

"Toward a Unitary Principle of Self," read at American Ontoanalytic Association Meeting, 5/71

"Recreation Phobia," *Recreation Management*, Volume 16, No. 3, 4/73

"The Role of a Psychiatrist in a University Health and Counseling Center," *Journal of the Florida Medical Association*, 10/73. Read at SE Conference on Counseling Personnel, St. Petersburg, FL, 10/73

Congress of Recreation and Parks (NPRA). Panel and workshop speaker with Jonathan Kozol and Margaret Mead. Topic: "Redefining Leisure," 10/73

"What is Existential Psychiatry?" Florida Psychiatric Society, Fall Meeting, 1975

"Sex and Love" [essay], presented to the Florida Psychiatric Association Annual Meeting, Tampa, FL, 11/82

"Mental and Emotional Illnesses Induced by Physical Trauma," Annual Meeting of the Clearwater Bar Association, Clearwater, FL, 4/85

Research and Survey Report for Health and Retirement Corporation of America on the need for a new Alzheimer's nursing home in Pinellas and Pasco Counties, FL, 3/87

"Bodyowners' Insurance: A Better Answer to the [Medical] Mispractice Crisis," *Florida Underwriter Magazine*, Vol. 7, #6, 6/90

"A Psychiatrist Talks About Love," *Psychiatric Times*, Summer, 1992

"Against Ambiguity: An Homage to Knowledgeable Love," *The Progressive Women's Quarterly*, Spring, 1993

"Obesity is Not a Psychiatric Illness," 45th Annual Symposium of the American Society of Bariatric Physicians, San Diego, CA, 11/16/95; and excerpted in PICOMESO (Pinellas County Medical Society) *Mailbag*, 2/96

Legislature Assignments
Rhode Island: Topic: Revision of the Rhode Island NGRI Statute
Florida: Topic: Revision of the Mentally Disordered Sex Offender Statute

Teaching
"Medical Psychology," Brown University Extension School, 1965
"The Psychology of Marriage," University of Rhode Island, 1970
"Group Psychodynamics," Brown University, 1971
"Psychodynamic Medicine" seminars with residents of Mariam and Rhode Island Hospitals, 1968–70
Psychiatric Supervisor of Psychology Ph.D. candidates, University of Rhode Island, 1968–70
Lecturer in "Abnormal Psychology" and "Leisure Studies," University of South Florida, Tampa, FL, 1972
Visiting faculty, St. Leo College, Brooksville, FL, "Personality Theory and the Criminal Mind," 1975–76
Lecturer in Neurophysiology, Argenbright International Institute of Polygraphy, St. Petersburg, FL, 5–7/85

Present Agenda of Expert Testimony
Physician Assisted Suicide, Florida Hemlock Society

Death Sentence Review, Office of the Capital Collateral Representative, Tampa, FL

Munchausen Syndrome by Proxy, Florida, New York, South Dakota and Iowa

NGRI and Aid in Sentencing [including several capital cases], Florida's Sixth Judicial
Circuit, Pinellas County

Mental Competency Evaluator, Florida Sixth Judicial Circuit

Media Experience

Frequent television and radio talk show appearances in Rhode Island and Florida

Featured contributor for articles on psychiatric issues in *Providence Journal* and *St.
Petersburg Times*

20/20 Show, consultant to producers, 1993

Guest, discussing Munchausen Syndrome (Disease) by Proxy and the cases he has
defended on the *Phil Donahue Show*, 5/14/92, https://www.youtube.com
/watch?v=rqLVA4FsBKs

Guest, discussing Munchausen Syndrome (Disease) by Proxy and the cases he has
defended, *Geraldo Rivera Show*, 5/25/93, https://www.youtube.com/watch?v
=HsVdSCnhUkM

Alfred E. Fireman MD, discusses Women's Rights and Delinquency on Ring Around
Rhode Island, in the mid 1960s, https://www.youtube.com/watch?v=w1imAHBe-VI

• • •

A Word from Payton Fireman, Dr. Fireman's Son

The resume/curriculum vitae above gives a structured sense of Alfred's accomplishments but comes
nowhere close to describing the passion and compassion
which he brought to his practice and his patients.

I remember Alfred rising early and leaving the
house before dawn, to go to the county jail. He went
to evaluate prisoners showing signs of mental illness
and to bring his skills to the most unfortunate and least
regarded. He used the first and best energies of his day
to treat the sick and the disordered in the dungeons of
our society. By his presence as witness, and with his
authority as a physician, he helped ensure that the mentally ill would not suffer more in jail because of their
infirmity. He stood guard in those places of misery to ameliorate the suffering and
reduce the trauma of jail time. Before he saw the people who could pay him, he brought
his skills to those who could not.

Alfred also had a great sense of humor as the accompanying picture clearly shows.